THE NEW MERMAIDS

The Roaring Girl

THE NEW MERMAIDS

General Editors
BRIAN MORRIS
Professor of English Literature, University of Sheffield

BRIAN GIBBONS
Senior Lecturer in English, University of York

ROMA GILL
Senior Lecturer in English Literature, University of Sheffield

The Roaring Girl

THOMAS MIDDLETON
AND THOMAS DEKKER

Edited by ANDOR GOMME
Senior Lecturer in English, University of Keele

LONDON/ERNEST BENN LIMITED

NEW YORK/W. W. NORTON & COMPANY INC.

First published in this form 1976
by Ernest Benn Limited
25 New Street Square, Fleet Street, London EC4A 3JA
& Sovereign Way, Tonbridge, Kent, TN9 1RW
and W. W. Norton and Company Inc.
500 Fifth Avenue, New York, N.Y. 10036

© *Ernest Benn Limited 1976*

Distributed in Canada by
The General Publishing Company Limited, Toronto

Printed in Great Britain

ISBN 0 510-34138-1 (*Paperback*)
ISBN 0-393-90024 x (U.S.A.)

TO

DOROTHY AND KEITH,

REBECCA, HUGH AND CHRISTA

CONTENTS

ACKNOWLEDGEMENTS

LIKE ALL STUDENTS of Middleton I have made extensive use of A. H. Bullen's fine edition of the *Works* (1885). I have also been helped by those of Alexander Dyce (1840), whose edition provided the basis for Bullen's and whose copy of *The Roaring Girl* in the original quarto I used as the copy-text, and of Havelock Ellis in the old Mermaid series (1887). J. P. Collier's edition of *The Roaring Girl* in the third edition of Dodsley's *Select Plays* (1825) and the recent textual edition by Fredson Bowers in volume III of his *Dramatic Works of Thomas Dekker* (1958) have likewise stimulated and informed me. I have dug deep into the work of Eric Partridge, in particular his *Shakespeare's Bawdy* (1956) and *Dictionary of Historical Slang* (Penguin edition, Harmondsworth, 1972), into E. H. Sugden's *Topographical Dictionary to the Works of Shakespeare and his Fellow Dramatists* (Manchester, 1925), and into M. P. Tilley's *Dictionary of the Proverbs in England in the Sixteenth and Seventeenth Centuries* (Ann Arbor, 1950). A. V. Judges's *The Elizabethan Underworld* (1930, recently reprinted) and E. D. Pendry's edition of a selection of Dekker's tracts (1967) were indispensable sources of information on cozenage and canting. The editors of *The Architectural Review* and Mr W. E. Godfrey generously allowed me to reproduce the drawing by W. H. Godfrey on p. xviii. Dr F. Celoria, Dr T. R. Henn, and Professor A. J. Smith kindly helped me by answering questions, and Dr Brian Gibbons has made a number of useful suggestions. I acknowledge with especial pleasure the help and encouragement given me by my colleagues Mr Francis Doherty and Mr Charles Swann, and above all by my wife, whose acuteness in nosing out villainy has been as invaluable as her keen eye for errors in typing and in print.

Keele,　　　　　　　　　　　　　　　　　　　　　　　　A.H.G.
November 1974

ABBREVIATIONS

1. *Texts of* The Roaring Girl

Q	the first edition (quarto), 1611.
Collier	J. P. Collier, ed., *Dodsley's Select Plays*, 3rd edn, 12 vols, VIII, 1825.
Dyce	A. Dyce, ed., *The Works of Thomas Middleton*, 5 vols, II, 1840.
Bullen	A. H. Bullen, ed., *The Works of Thomas Middleton*, 8 vols, IV, 1885.
Ellis	Havelock Ellis, ed., *Thomas Middleton*, The Mermaid Series, 2 vols, II, 1887.
Bowers	Fredson Bowers, ed., *The Dramatic Works of Thomas Dekker*, 4 vols, III, 1958.

2. *Other works*

Bald (Chronology)	R. C. Bald, 'The Chronology of Middleton's Plays', *Modern Language Review*, XXXII (1937), 33–43.
Chambers	E. K. Chambers, *The Elizabethan Stage*, 4 vols, 1923.
Greg	W. W. Greg, *A Bibliography of the English Printed Drama to the Restoration*, 4 vols, 1939–50.
Judges	A. V. Judges, *The Elizabethan Underworld*, 1930.
OED	*The Oxford English Dictionary*.
Price (Manuscript and Quarto)	George R. Price, 'The Manuscript and Quarto of *The Roaring Girl*', *The Library* (Fifth series), XI (1956), 182–3.
Price (Shares)	George R. Price, 'The Shares of Middleton and Dekker in a Collaborated Play', *Papers from the Michigan Academy of Arts and Sciences*, XXX (1945), 601–15.
Sh. Bawdy	Eric Partridge, *Shakespeare's Bawdy*, 1956.
Sh. Eng.	Walter Ralegh, etc., eds, *Shakespeare's England*, 2 vols, Oxford, 1917.
Sugden	E. H. Sugden, *A Topographical Dictionary to the Works of Shakespeare and his Fellow Dramatists*, Manchester, 1925.
Tilley	M. P. Tilley, *A Dictionary of the Proverbs in England in the Sixteenth and Seventeenth Centuries*, Ann Arbor, 1950.

Whiting   B. J. Whiting, *Proverbs, Sentences, and Proverbial Phrases from English Writings mainly before 1500* (Cambridge, Mass., and London, 1968).

3. *Journals*
E in C   *Essays in Criticism*
MLR   *Modern Language Review*
N & Q   *Notes and Queries*
RES   *Review of English Studies*
SP   *Studies in Philology*

4. *Other abbreviations*
ed.   this edition
qu.   quoted by or in
sc.   to wit
s.d.   stage direction
s.p.   speech prefix
SR   Stationers' Register
stet Q   Q says this, and it may stand.

INTRODUCTION

THE AUTHORS

THOMAS MIDDLETON was born in London in 1580, the son of William Middleton, a bricklayer of substance who carried arms and owned property in Shoreditch and Limehouse. He was baptized at St Lawrence Jewry on 18 April.[1] William Middleton died in January 1585, and his widow Anne was soon remarried to an impoverished but ambitious grocer named Thomas Harvey, who had gambled and lost everything as a member of Ralegh's and Grenville's abortive expedition to Roanoke Island, also in 1585. Harvey's principal aim seems to have been to get his hands on the Middleton property; this also appears to have been the reason for Allen Waterer's marriage in 1596 to Avice Middleton, Thomas's sister. Until 1603, by which time both Anne Harvey and Waterer were dead, legal squabbles over the properties disrupted the family; even after her first husband's death, Avice and her second husband, John Empson, took up litigation, still over the property, against Waterer's brother. Middleton himself probably married about 1602, for his son Edward was nineteen in 1623. His wife was the granddaughter of the composer and organist John Marbeck, and her brother was for a time an actor with the Admiral's Men, for whose successors Middleton wrote with Dekker. She was probably the Maulyn Marbeck who was christened on 9 July 1575 at St Dunstan's in the West; this agrees with the name of the playwright's widow, given as Magdalen, who applied in February 1628 for a gift of money from the City of London and was granted twenty nobles.

When he was seventeen, Middleton published his first work, *The Wisdom of Solomon Paraphrased* (1597), which is exceedingly long and has been found by most of its few readers exceedingly tedious. He matriculated at Queen's College, Oxford in April 1598, and although in 1600 he sold his share of the family property to his brother-in-law Waterer so that he could stay there, he had to return to London to help his mother in one of her lawsuits in 1601 and apparently did not graduate. He was then said to have been seen

---

[1] I have drawn for this account on the published narratives of R. H. Barker, M. Eccles, and D. M. Holmes, and have helped myself liberally to Alan Brissenden's brief account of Middleton's life in the New Mermaid edition of *A Chaste Maid in Cheapside* (1968).

in London 'daily accompanying the players'.[2] By 1602 he is recorded
by Henslowe as collaborating with Munday, Drayton, and Webster
on the now lost play *Caesar's Fall*, and in the same year had probably
written his own earliest plays, *Blurt Master Constable* (not certainly
his), *The Phoenix*, and *The Family of Love*. These are plays of somewhat mixed genre, with satirical and popular elements combined,
but *The Family of Love* begins the splendid series of satiric comedies
of London life which Middleton wrote through the decade, including *A Mad World, My Masters* and *Michaelmas Term* (1604), *Your
Five Gallants* (1605), *A Trick to Catch the Old One* (1606), *A Chaste
Maid in Cheapside* (1613), and perhaps others that have been lost.[3]
Most of these plays were written for the children's companies,
chiefly Paul's Boys; but by 1604 Middleton was also working (with
Dekker) for Prince Henry's Men at the Fortune on the first part of
The Honest Whore, and for them in about 1608 *The Roaring Girl*
was also written. The children's companies were disbanded in 1606,
and thereafter Middleton wrote for Lady Elizabeth's company at
the Swan (*A Chaste Maid*), but chiefly for the King's Men at the
Globe.[4]

The plays which Middleton wrote after about 1613, alone or in
collaboration with William Rowley, show a continuing interest in
the exploration of character—especially women's—which is already
notable in the two plays written with Dekker. To this group belong
More Dissemblers Besides Women, No Wit, No Help, like a Woman's,
and *A Fair Quarrel*, and they point forward to the two great tragedies of the early 1620s, *The Changeling* (with Rowley) and *Women
Beware Women*, which last has recently also been seen as the horrific
culmination of the satiric vision of the city comedies.[5] Middleton's
dramatic range is further demonstrated by the strange parody-
tragedy of *The Mayor of Queenborough* and several romances
(including *The Widow* and *The Witch*) somewhat in the manner of
Fletcher. His last known play was the brilliant political satire *A
Game at Chess* (1624), one of the most sensational dramatic successes

---

[2] See P. G. Phialas, 'Middleton's Early Contact with the Law', *SP*, LII
(1955), 186–94.

[3] The dates are those given in R. C. Bald's 'The Chronology of Middleton's
Plays', *MLR*, XXXII (1937), 33–43.

[4] Middleton has been strongly urged as the author of *The Revenger's Tragedy*,
published in 1607, but if he was, it stands apart from his other known work
of the time, even if its satiric tragedy gives it a link with the much later
Women Beware Women.

[5] See R. B. Parker, 'Middleton's Experiments with Comedy and Judgment'
in Brown and Harris, eds, *Jacobean Theatre* (Stratford-upon-Avon Studies I,
1960), 179–200, esp. 192ff,

of all time, which ran for nine successive days at the Globe and was only stopped by the protest of the Spanish ambassador. Middleton and the players were summoned before the Privy Council, but no action was taken when he failed to appear and his son Edward was called to answer for him.

During the period when the theatres were closed for a year because of the violent outbreak of plague (1603–04) Middleton, like other playwrights, turned to pamphleteering and wrote *Father Hubburd's Tales* and *The Black Book*. He was later responsible for a a number of city masques and pageants, the first being for the installation of his namesake Sir Thomas Middleton as Lord Mayor in 1613: it is not known if there was any blood relationship. In 1620 Middleton was appointed City Chronologer, a post whose duties he performed with exactness until his death: he was succeeded by Ben Jonson (who had classed him, among many others, as a base fellow). There is evidence that he held other occasional official posts. Middleton died in 1627 and was buried on 4 July at St Mary's, Newington Butts, near which he had lived for some years. His wife survived him by only a year.

Rather little is known of the life of Thomas Dekker. He was born probably about 1572 in London. His early life is a complete blank, though there is a tradition that he trailed a pike in the Low Countries: he certainly seems to have known Dutch and enjoyed bringing snippets of it into his plays; his name suggests a possible Dutch origin. He first appears in Henslowe's diary in 1598, most notably on 4 February when Henslowe 'lent unto the companey . . . to disecharge Mr. Dicker owt of the cownter in the powltrey, the some of fortie shillings'. This may have been the first, but it was not the last, acquaintance that Dekker had with prisons, and he seems to have been constantly in financial difficulties. He was perhaps working for the Admiral's Men as early as 1594, certainly by 1598.[6] In a single year from April 1599 to March 1600 he is recorded as being engaged on fourteen plays; but this activity is in large measure to be accounted for by the extent of his collaboration with other dramatists, who are known to have included Jonson, Drayton, Chettle, Haughton, Wilson, Day, and later Webster, Middleton, Massinger, Marston, Ford, and the two Rowleys. Much of his work for Henslowe was evidently hackwork, and only three of the earliest plays have survived, *Old Fortunatus*, *Patient Grissel*, and the immensely popular *Shoemakers' Holiday* (originally named *The Gentle Craft*). By 1602 he had had a hand in about forty-four plays.

[6] See E. K. Chambers, *The Elizabethan Stage* (Oxford, 1923), III, 289.

He was at this time engaged with Jonson and Marston in the war of the theatres, which he himself christened the Poetomachia. Jonson ridiculed him in *Poetaster* as Demetrius, the playdresser and plagiary, whose 'doublet's a little decayed: he is otherwise a simple honest fellow'. Dekker's answer in *Satiromastix* (probably written with Marston), where Jonson is entertainingly mocked as Horace, the laborious poet, is much better-humoured. Indeed Dekker is spoken of constantly as a man of kindliness, cheerfulness, and charm, with 'poetry enough for anything'. Jonson, however, seems always to have treated him sourly, despite which they were engaged together on the coronation devices which celebrated James I's entry into London in 1604.

The Honest Whore, the first part written with Middleton in 1604, the second probably alone soon afterwards, is widely agreed to be Dekker's most considerable play: it is a curious amalgam of traditional popular comedy, savage farce, and sentimental morality; in the shopkeeper scenes it looks forward to Dekker's engagement in citizen comedy, first with Webster in *Westward Ho!* and *Northward Ho!*—knockabout medleys of lechery, thieving, and old-fashioned honesty, which were burlesqued in Jonson, Chapman, and Marston's *Eastward Ho!*—and then again with Middleton in *The Roaring Girl*. This was also the period of his most active pamphleteering: his prose tracts are many, lively and delightful, giving an unrivalled picture of London life of the time, which makes Dekker the true heir of Nashe. The first of note was *The Wonderful Year* (1603),

> wherein is shewed the picture of London lying sick of the Plague. At the end of all (like a merry Epilogue to a dull Play) certain tales are cut out in sundry fashions of purpose to shorten the lives of long winter's nights, that lie watching in the dark for us

—characteristic in its desire to lighten the grimness of the time. *The Seven Deadly Sins of London* (1606) begins his best-known group of tracts, which includes *The Bellman of London* and *Lanthorn and Candlelight* (1608) and the brilliant *Gull's Horn-Book* of 1609, full, among other things, of entertaining and useful information about the Jacobean theatre.

In 1613 Dekker was imprisoned for debt in the King's Bench Prison, where he stayed for six years. No plays are known from this period, which is most notable for the production of *The Four Birds of Noah's Ark*, a book of prayers in which his deep vein of piety is expressed in devotional prose of remarkable eloquence. The King's Bench seems, as Miss Bradbrook says, to have quenched Dekker's delicate fancy and rough vitality. The comedy in his later plays, *Match Me in London* and *The Wonder of a Kingdom*, has little real gaiety and on occasion even turns a little sour. The former is called on the title-page a tragi-comedy, and this seems to have been Dekker's preferred vein in what was apparently the last decade of his life and includes *The Virgin Martyr*, written with Massinger, and *The Witch of Edmonton*, with Ford and Rowley. The mixture of hands and modes in both plays is bizarre, and Dekker's contributions have not been fully determined. His last years are almost as obscure as his first: he died probably in 1632, being, it seems, buried on 25 August in Clerkenwell, where a recusant of his name was recorded in 1626 and 1628.

SOURCE AND DATE

The Roaring Girl has really no source outside the authors' observation and imagination, except for the stimulus offered by the real Moll, from whose character and habits Moll in the play takes off but departs largely. Most of our knowledge of Moll Frith comes from *The Life and Death of Mrs Mary Frith. Commonly called Mal Cutpurse*, an anonymous pamphlet published, evidently soon after her death, in 1662. According to this tract she was born in 1589, but the real date seems likely to have been several years earlier,[7] for she was plainly well known by 1605 when it is recorded in the *Consistory of London Correction Book* that Mary Frith confessed before the Court that 'being at a play about three quarters of a year since at the Fortune in mans apparel' she had uttered various 'immodest and lascivious speaches . . . and also sat upon the stage in the public viewe of all the people there present in mans apparel and played upon her lute and sange a song'.[8] Chambers suggested that this is the occasion referred to in the much-discussed lines in the Epilogue of the play (ll. 33–6)—

> if what both have done
> Cannot full pay your expectation,
> The Roaring Girl herself, some few days hence,
> Shall on this stage give larger recompense.

But this cannot be prophetic of a single extempore performance: it is possible, of course, that Mary Frith did this sort of thing quite

---

[7] The writer of the tract says that she was seventy-three when she died (her habit of smoking was thought to have contributed to her longevity: O tempora, o mores), and there is evidence that this was before Charles II's return to London in May 1660, to celebrate which happy event she apparently left £20 in her will that the conduit by St Bride's might run with wine.

[8] See E. K. Chambers, 'Elizabethan Stage Gleanings', *RES*, I (1925), 77–8.

often, but there is no independent evidence of her having acted. She is, however, known to have done penance at Paul's Cross early in 1612, showing every sign of contrition and weeping bitterly, but it was afterward suspected that 'she was maudlin-drunk, being discovered to have tippled off three quarts of sack before she came to her penance'.[9] Her offence on this occasion is not known, but from her youth she was of a boisterous, masculine spirit—in the words of the anonymous life

> a very Tomrig or Rumpscuttle she was, and delighted and sported only in boys' play and pastime, not minding or companying with the girls: many a bang and blow this hoyting procured her, but she was not so to be tamed or taken off from her rude inclinations; she could not endure their sedentary life of sewing or stitching; a sampler was as grievous as a winding-sheet; her needle, bodkin, and thimble she could not think on quietly, wishing them changed into sword and dagger for a bout at cudgels.

Not surprisingly an attempt to put her out to service was a failure; it was then that she started wearing male clothes which to her dying day she would never leave off. She is said to have been the first woman 'who vindicated for her sex the right of smoking'.

There seems good evidence that—unlike Moll's in the play—her skill with sword and cudgel was not always put to godly ends, and in later years she was notorious as a whore, bawd, cutpurse, and receiver, a female Moriarty keeping a gang of thieves in her service. These are just what our Moll is falsely accused of by all who take the common report for truth, and in the play she is given two separate defences of her reputation (III.i, 86ff. and V.i, 289ff.). In the Epistle to the Readers Middleton makes the point again that 'worse things . . . the world has taxed her for, than has been written of her', though his continuation—' 'tis the excellency of a writer to leave things better than he finds 'em'—is ambiguous. It seems plausible to suppose that *The Roaring Girl* was what prompted Thomas Freeman to write his epigram on her (published in *Rubbe and a Great Cast* in 1614, but perhaps written some years earlier):

> They say Moll's honest, and it may be so,
> But yet it is a shrewd suspicion no:
> To touch but pitch, 'tis known it will defile;
> Moll wears the breech, what may she be the while?
> Sure she that doth the shadow so much grace,
> What will she when the substance comes in place?

It is precisely the roaring girl's triumphant claim that she has touched

[9] Letter from John Chamberlain to Dudley Carleton, 11 February 1612, quoted by Bullen, IV, 4.

pitch and not been defiled. Freeman is reasserting the reliability of
the 'common voice' (against which Moll has constantly to fight)—
and it seems, so far as the real woman goes, with justice.

Mary Frith was a popular figure in her time and appears, in one
form or another, in a number of contemporary writings. The Stationers' Register of August 1610 contains 'A Booke called the Madde
Prancks of Merry Mall of the Bankside, with her Walks in Mans
Apparel and to what Purpose. Written by John Day'. No copy of this
has survived, and it may never have been printed: it was perhaps a
play, but may well have been a prose tract. Bullen remarks that he
would be sorry to think that this is the 'foul book' alluded to in the
Epilogue of *The Roaring Girl* (ll. 22–3), but Bald[10] has argued
plausibly that it is much more likely to be a lost pamphlet by 'S.R.'
(the author of the abusive *Martin Mark-All*), to which Dekker refers
in the opening address of *Lanthorn and Candlelight*. Nathan Field's
play *Amends for Ladies*, written probably in 1612, brings Mall
Cutpurse in for a brief scene in which she shows herself to be an
aggressive bawd, attempting (with no success) to undermine the
virtue of Grace Seldom, who shows her off in language which recalls Sir Alexander's view of Moll at the start of *The Roaring Girl*
(I.ii, 125ff.), but is in tone akin to Moll's own spurning of her would-
be seducer:

> Hence lewd impudent
> I know not what to term thee, man or woman,
> For nature shaming to acknowledge thee
> For either, hath produced thee to the world
> Without a sex; some say thou art a woman,
> Others a man, and many thou art both
> Woman and man, but I think rather neither
> Or man and horse, as the old centaurs were feigned.[11]

Field seems to have been capitalizing on the success of *The Roaring
Girl*, which he evidently knew; and in 1639, when the second quarto
of his play was published, she was still popular enough for it to be
worth while to bring her name on to the title-page.

An interesting sidelight on Mary Frith's activities, with a direct
bearing on a small episode in the play, came to light in 1934 when
Margaret Dowling published an account of a suit of complaint of
wrongful arrest and imprisonment brought in the Court of Star
Chamber in 1621 against several people including 'Mary Markham

---

[10] art. cit., 38–9.
[11] See *The Plays of Nathan Field*, ed. William Peery (Austin, Texas, 1950),
177. Peery finds the scene to be without artistic justification.

alias Frith, *alias* Thrift, *alias* "Malcutpurse" '.[12] During a lengthy series of (evidently false) accusations, Margaret Dell was brought before Mary Markham, who, objected to by Margaret's husband as being 'a notorious infamous person, and such a one as was well known & acquainted with all thieves & cutpurses', asserted very angrily 'that she had a royal commission to examine all such persons, and advised Dell to go before he was beaten'. Later, in her own defence, Mary Markham described how a man claiming to have been robbed

> became to this defendant and desired her to do her endeavour to try if she could by any means find out the pickpocket or help him to his money, he being before of this defendant's acquaintance and having heard how by this defendant's means many that had had their purses cut or goods stolen had been helped to their goods again and divers of the offenders taken or discovered,

though there is no further mention of a royal warrant. She admits that in reply to ill words or language she 'might and did give them some reply in some tart or angry manner again'. Mary Frith evidently carried power in the underworld for many years, for it must be to incidents of this kind that Dekker alludes at V.i, 279ff., when Moll, having exposed a cutpurse, warns him imperiously to make sure of the return of some stolen money and is instantly obeyed:

> Heart, there's a knight to whom I'm bound for many favours lost his purse at the last new play i'the Swan, seven angels in't: make it good, you're best; do you see? no more.

This little incident, then, is taken closely from the real Moll Frith's activities, but for the most part Moll is, as Professor Bradbrook says, not a portrait from life. D. M. Holmes[13] seems to me to identify the two Molls much too closely, for the 'heroic quality' he rightly sees in the heroine of the play and the 'dignified self-knowledge which her rejection of a rich suitor implies'[14] are quite absent from the known sources of information about Mary Frith, of whom Holmes observes that her nickname (i.e., Moll Cutpurse) 'makes it clear that at some time in her career she was a criminal'. But Moll is deliberately given the opportunity to explain that. More interesting is the other nickname which gives the play its title and which Moll jestingly assumes when she is rather grimly teasing Sir Alexander in the last scene (V.ii, 154–61). The roaring

[12] See Margaret Dowling, 'A Note on Moll Cutpurse—"The Roaring Girl" ', *RES*, X (1934), 67–71.
[13] *The Art of Thomas Middleton: a Critical Study* (Oxford, 1970), 101.
[14] M. C. Bradbrook, *The Growth and Structure of Elizabethan Comedy*, 2nd edn (1973), 163.

boys of the early seventeenth century were swaggering bucks given to riotous and quarrelsome behaviour to show off their virility. There is some roaring in *Amends for Ladies;* and in Middleton and Rowley's *A Fair Quarrel* there are two scenes in which Chough and Trimtram go to a roaring school to learn to quarrel 'unfairly'. But the best-known would-be roarer is Kastril, the angry boy in *The Alchemist*, who 'is come up to learn to quarrel, and to live by his wits' (II.vi, 60–1) and tells Face

> I have heard some speech
> Of the angry boys, and seen 'em take tobacco,
> And in his shop: and I can take it too.
> And I would fain be one of 'em, and go down
> And practise i'the country.   (III.iv, 21–5)

Moll is certainly quick to take action and sometimes offence, always ready with a tart answer. In II.i, after Mistress Openwork has been causelessly rude and abrupt to her, Moll's 'spleen's up' (II.i, 220), though quickly assuaged by the fortuitous appearance of a fellow who has abused her and whom she can cudgel. But her quarrels are not unprompted; she is really a very different person from her namesake and prototype.[15]

Mary Frith's likely date of birth gives us reason to suppose that *The Roaring Girl* was written not very long before 1611 when the quarto was published. F. G. Fleay[16] puts the date of composition as early as 1604, because of the allusion (IV.ii, 123) to *Westward Ho!*, which is known to have been written in that year. But as Bullen observed, this proves nothing, for the allusion 'would have been quite as intelligible to the audience in 1611 as in 1604'.[17] Chambers supports an early date because of the evidence he discovered of Mary Frith's appearance on the Fortune stage, but, as I have argued above, the lines in the Epilogue cannot point forward to a single instance of the kind of act she confessed to having put on. On the other hand, the title-page describes the play as having 'lately beene acted on the Fortune-Stage'—a vague phrase admittedly and not necessarily referring to the first performance, which in any case need not have followed immediately on its composition. (Fleay indeed thinks that Dekker revised it just before publication; but if this were so, would he not have done something about the controversial lines in the Epilogue if they really point to an event of seven years before?) Bald argues for a date of 1607 or 1608: he points out the marked

---

[15] For the sources of Dekker's acquaintance with thieves' cant, see Appendix, pp. 146ff.
[16] *A Biographical Chronicle of the English Drama, 1559–1642* (1891), I, 132.
[17] op. cit., I, xxxv.

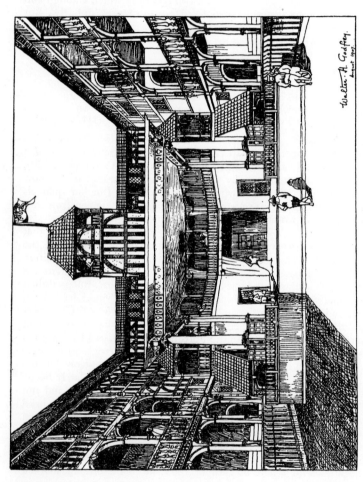

The Fortune Theatre, London. Restoration, as indicated in the original
specification, by Walter H. Godfrey

similarity between the canting scene and parts of *The Bellman of London*, which was entered in the Stationers' Register on 14 March 1608—a relationship 'so close . . . as to suggest that Dekker was working on the play and the pamphlet at about the same time'.[18] (There are, however, one or two cant words in the scene which seem not to have been included in any of Dekker's tracts before the third edition of *Lanthorn and Candlelight* (see Appendix, p. 146), which included a supplement expanding and silently correcting earlier material. But corrections could have been made to the play itself, especially if Bowers is right[19] that a fair text was specially prepared for printing. (Bald also suggests that the now lost pamphlet by 'S.R.' mentioned above (p. xv) would help towards a date of 1608, if indeed it is the 'foul book' adverted to; and as a final piece of evidence Bald points to the lines where Moll's ability to draw the crowds is likened to that of a comet:

> let this strange thing walk, stand or sit,
> No blazing star draws more eyes after it.   (I.ii, 133)

'Halley's comet reached its perihelion towards the end of November 1607 and must have been visible when Dekker was writing *The Bellman of London*'.[20]) There seems good reason to accept Bald's date, with the possibility of amendments made shortly before printing.

THE PLAY

The revival of interest in Jacobean comedy has largely passed *The Roaring Girl* by. The play was included in the old Mermaid selection of Middleton in 1887 when Swinburne put it in its place as 'well written and well contrived and fairly diverting—especially to an idle or an uncritical reader'.[21] Forty years later Eliot's praise was much less guarded: '*The Roaring Girl* . . . is typical of the comedies of Middleton, and it is the best . . . a great play . . . for the reason that Middleton was a great observer of human nature, without fear, without sentiment, without prejudice'.[22] This estimate has been widely regarded as extravagant, and *The Roaring Girl* has dropped back into obscurity.

[18] art. cit., 38.
[19] Fredson Bowers, *The Dramatic Works of Thomas Dekker*, III (1958), 8.
[20] Bald, art. cit., 38.
[21] *Thomas Middleton*, ed. Havelock Ellis, with an introduction by A. C. Swinburne, 2 vols, 1887.
[22] T. S. Eliot, 'Thomas Middleton' (*Elizabethan Essays*, 1927), in *Selected Essays*, 2nd edn (1934), 166, 169.

Its neglect may be due in some measure to its being in one aspect—and that the most memorable—not at all typical of Middleton's comedies, or of Dekker's. Certainly there is a good deal of familiar material: Middleton reworks his jokes and re-establishes the commonplaces on which Jacobean comedy leant so heavily. As L. C. Knights drily remarked, here as elsewhere 'we find—exciting discovery!—that gallants are likely to be in debt, that they make love to citizens' wives, that lawyers are concerned more for their profits than for justice, and that cutpurses are thieves'.[23] Knights goes on to assert that 'Middleton tells us nothing at all about these as *individuals* in a particular place and period . . . And the obvious reason, it seems to me, is that he was not interested in doing so'. This may well be partially true of most of Middleton's comedies, though I find his large figures more memorable than Knights does and the lack of individualization is not necessarily a condemnation; but in *The Roaring Girl* it is not only the figure of Moll herself which sets the play apart from its contemporaries. That the citizens are on the whole treated genially may show the hand, and doubtless at least the influence, of Dekker, especially towards the end: they are quite unlike the gigantic caricature figures of Quomodo or Hoard or Yellowhammer,[24] and are in fact observed with some shrewd discrimination. A little of the same interest in what differentiates even one scoundrel from another is visible among the portraits of the gallants and even in that of the principal old grasper himself: there is something in Dorothy Farr's view[25] that *The Roaring Girl* is, like *The Honest Whore*, 'concerned not only with citizen life but with the struggles and perplexities of recognizable human beings in a society as harsh as it was lively'.

The play has, however, much in common with those other comedies, now rather better known, which Middleton wrote on his own in the first decade of the seventeenth century. Several plots are run together, though the connection between the main one, involving Sebastian Wengrave and his father, and the intrigues among the gallants and citizens is very thin, coming only from Moll's more or less accidental engagement with Laxton. The loose construction of the play allows by compensation much social mobility and a rather wider range of 'character portraits' than we find in most citizen comedy. Yet the machinery of *The Roaring Girl* is of a familiar kind: tricks are sprung (the main plot culminates in a trick to catch

[23] L. C. Knights, *Drama and Society in the Age of Jonson* (1937), 258.
[24] In, respectively, *Michaelmas Term*, *A Trick to Catch the Old One*, and *A Chaste Maid in Cheapside*.
[25] Dorothy M. Farr, *Thomas Middleton and the Drama of Realism* (Edinburgh, 1973), 3.

the old one), intrigues are attempted and rebound to discomfit the intriguers, disguise of many kinds is constantly turned to, and most of the chief characters adopt temporary roles for special purposes. Middleton's 'dominant driving purpose' (as Brian Gibbons calls it[26]) may be felt to lie behind and explain this trickery, as in the other plays, though the technique by which it is turned to account works quite differently, essentially because the world of *The Roaring Girl* is no longer the completely amoral one of *A Trick to Catch the Old One* or *Michaelmas Term*, in which the enactment of a moral purpose depends altogether on the irony of self-inflicted retributions: among the gallants and the citizens' wives and the old misers move figures whose directness of moral statement and clarity of intention stand out all the sharplier for being set against the devious self-seeking trickery of the rest.

There is, however, a further distinction to be drawn. R. B. Parker begins his essay on Middleton's comedies with the observation that

> at the heart of Middleton's very personal comic style is a tension between skill in the presentation of manners and a desire to denounce immorality. The very brilliance of his manners comedy, with its ingenious intrigue, verbal wit, and vivid representation of contemporary London scenes and behaviour, is apt to obscure his concern with deprecation.[27]

To this *The Roaring Girl* is an exception, and not only because of the speeches of Moll and others roundly denouncing vice, some of which, before they descend to moralistic *sententiae*, show moral fervour and even passion. In such plays as *Michaelmas Term* or *A Chaste Maid*, it is impossible to escape the sense of delight that Middleton shows in the ingenuities by which completely unscrupulous people gain their ends (perhaps only temporarily) and defeat their rivals: the moral purpose—it is this above all which marks Middleton as of the school, if not the tribe, of Ben—is enacted silently, by satiric implication: trickery must itself be read as a sign of the corruption of deceit and self-seeking, yet Middleton, like Jonson, depends on the fun of the complex intrigue to hold the attention and interest of an audience whose feelings are likely to be disturbed or even confused by such a scene as the seduction of Mrs Harebrain in *A Mad World, My Masters*; for not only is the trickery involved clever and amusing, but Harebrain is a complacent ass who seems to ask to be ridiculed; yet (as is plain from the repentance speech afterwards) we are not expected to approve the adultery; or, if we do condone it at the time, we find ourselves hoist later. In *The Roaring Girl* this tension has

[26] Brian Gibbons, *Jacobean City Comedy* (1968), 106.
[27] R. B. Parker, art. cit., 179.

gone: the abundant trickery is now largely used for ends which the audience can be openly invited to approve—witness Moll's assignment with Laxton (II.i), Master Openwork's deception of Goshawk (II.i), and the involved series of stratagems which eventually traps Sir Alexander into not only agreeing to Sebastian's marriage with Mary but richly endowing it as well. In each of these intrigues a villain—so thoroughly objectionable and unpleasant that we can all cheer when he gets his comeuppance—is exposed and discomfited: the method may be akin to the devices of the cozeners in the other comedies, but the agent is in each case one in whose moral uprightness we can be comfortably secure. So the trick is blessed by the end to which it is put; and the only stratagem of which this is not true—Mistress Gallipot's device for getting money to Laxton (III.ii)—has by contrast a decidedly sour air: there is no enjoyment in her success. So not only is virtue victorious in *The Roaring Girl* (the appalling triumph of Allwit at the end of *A Chaste Maid* would be unthinkable here), but it is also seen to be delightful and vice ugly. This makes *The Roaring Girl* on the whole a good-humoured, cheerful, and even sunny play, in which there is much unaffected, if rather simple, enjoyment: the citizens are plainly going to have a jolly time at Parlous Pond (II.i), and Lord Noland means it when he says to Jack Dapper and his companions (V.i, 55), 'Here's such a merry ging, I could find in my heart to sail to the world's end with such company'. The chief rogue turns out to be only pretending, and all criminals are very easily disarmed by Moll.

Doubtless Dekker's influence is responsible for softening the characteristic acerbity of Middleton's satiric humour. The play seems deliberately to attempt a fusion of the two principal streams into which, as Miss Bradbrook points out, English comedy had divided in about 1600: 'On the one hand, the popular domestic themes handled in sanguine and traditional ways: on the other, themes equally traditional, but handled in ways which were melancholic and satiric'.[28] Dr G. R. Price, in his essay on the shares of the two authors in the play, remarks that 'contrasting a romance with an action of cynical and realistic humor is characteristic of Middleton'.[29] But in most of Middleton's comedies the romance is treated very briskly and true love simply taken for granted. *The Roaring Girl*, on the other hand, begins with Mary, the lovelorn and apparently deserted girl, lamenting her sad state in words which, though they may seem to be those of merely formal or conventional complaint,

[28] Bradbrook, op. cit., 119.
[29] George R. Price, 'The Shares of Middleton and Dekker in a Collaborated Play', *Papers from the Michigan Academy of Arts and Sciences*, XXX (1945), 606.

reveal by implication the feeling against which superficial or interested association and intrigue are judged:

> Love woven slightly
> (Such as thy false heart makes) wears out as lightly,
> But love being truly bred i'th'soul (like mine)
> Bleeds even to death, at the least wound it takes.   (I.i, 29)

In these lines, Miss Bradbrook says, 'the adage that the body is the garment of the soul underlies the implied contrast between love bred in the one and in the other; but the paradox, which follows logically, that the soul bleeds (and the body merely frays) gives an echoing depth to the passage'.[30] Mary is not on the stage long or often enough to make this really palpable on her own; but it is confirmed by her association with Moll, whose vigour and forthrightness of statement and action guarantee not only decency but soundness and depth of feeling in a more direct way. The doubling of the name is a deliberate, if elementary, device to establish the identity of purpose in the two, demonstrated finally when Moll 'impersonates' Mary in the last scene in order to complete the trick which secures Mary's happiness.[31]

The moral stance of *The Roaring Girl* is—thanks largely to one or two powerful speeches of Moll herself—much more explicit than in Middleton's other city comedies, and gives less occasion to reflect on his 'equivocal view of life' which a number of writers have either complained of or delighted in.[32] The pose which he assumes in, for example, *A Trick* or *A Chaste Maid*, that vice is not simply the common temper of the age but man's natural element, is, though the gallants form an exceptionally nasty group, abandoned. From the start we are indeed offered generalizations about the degeneracy of the age, but the speakers are those, such as Sir Davy Dapper—'Good tales do well/In these bad days, where vice does so excel' (I.ii, 61)—who are not only complacent but, as we discover, mean and spiteful as well. So the statements are undercut; and such a performance as Master Openwork's rebuke of Goshawk (IV.ii, 203ff.), though framed in conventionally cynical terms, sees wrongdoing as weakness rather than vice and accompanies the exposure with a somewhat self-satisfied offer of forgiveness and an invitation to dinner. There is much here to suggest that sentimental morality of Dekker's which led Miss Bradbrook to complain that 'in his easy pity and boundless tolerance, [he] appears something of a moral

---

[30] op. cit., 155.
[31] See further below, pp. xxxv-xxxvi.
[32] Middleton has both been called a Puritan (by Parker) and said to have no moral position at all (by Dunkel).

sloven'.[33] Yet, as if to stiffen these self-indulgent tendencies, even apparently straightforward moral statements and situations are sometimes undermined by a joke or a dubiously suggestive piece of something near perversity as when Sebastian, united with Mary by Moll on the assurance that their loves are honest—for she would 'scorn to make such shift to bring you together else'—discovers a peculiar relish in kissing Mary in male clothing:

> As some have a conceit their drink tastes better
> In an outlandish cup than in our own,
> So methinks every kiss she gives me now
> In this strange form, is worth a pair of two.   (IV.i, 54)

And earlier Moll herself, kindly but firmly and 'with the dignity of self-knowledge' rejecting Sebastian's seemingly genuine advances, turns her straightforward honesty into a merry quip on her own habit of going dressed as a man:

> Sir, I am so poor to requite you, you must look for nothing but thanks of me: I have no humour to marry . . . I love you so well, sir, for your good will I'd be loath you should repent your bargain after, and therefore we'll ne'er come together at first. I have the head now of myself, and am man enough for a woman . . .
>
> (II.ii, 35)[34]

Such moments qualify, though they do not really obscure, the moral openness of *The Roaring Girl*, an openness which gives the sanguine cheerfulness of the play roots without which it might seem fatuous.

Openness may seem a strange feature to stress when talking of a play in which so many characters, for good or bad ends, assume disguises, play roles, and seem to be other than they are. In fact the age-old theme of the contrast between appearance and reality, of the danger of being deceived by surfaces and the consequent need to penetrate to reality beneath, does give a theme to the somewhat haphazard collection of characters, events, and episodes which make up the play: such unity as it has resides not in a tight interweaving of plots as in the much denser and more ingeniously contrived *Chaste Maid*, but in the demonstration that the same kind of deception and scheming is found everywhere and can always be unmasked by plain dealing. When Sebastian is reaffirming his plan to trick his father by seeming to make love to Moll (II.ii, 191), he

[33] op. cit., 125. The scene in question is almost certainly Dekker's. See below, p. xxxiii.

[34] The opening of this speech recalls Hamlet's answer, in very different circumstances, to Rosencrantz and Guildenstern when they come to visit him: 'Beggar that I am, I am even poor in thanks' (II.ii, 275)—one among several reminiscences visible in the play.

says, 'plain dealing in this world takes no effect'. But ultimately, in *The Roaring Girl*, it always does: the truth is revealed by direct challenge and openness. So Mistress Openwork, bemused by and half-believing Goshawk's slanders, is nevertheless true to her name, challenges her husband openly, and the two are quickly reconciled; yet the episode itself was started by Openwork's professing to be what he was not (a whoremaster) and putting his supposed friend to a test. 'I pray', asks Master Gallipot, when Greenwit, the false sumner, has been unmasked, 'who plays a knack to know an honest man in this company?' (IV.ii, 266). And the answer seems to be: those who know the ways of deception. In his boastful speech about his gallery, Sir Alexander tells of how, among the rest of the pictured scene,

> a cutpurse thrusts and leers
> With hawk's eyes for his prey: I need not show him,
> By a hanging villainous look yourselves may know him.
> (I.ii, 26)

But when real cutpurses come on the scene, 'very gallant', they fool the young gentlemen completely, and it is only Moll who sees through them, because as she explains,

> In younger days, when I was apt to stray,
> I have sat amongst such adders; seen their stings,
> As any here might, and in full playhouses
> Watched their quick-diving hands, to bring to shame
> Such rogues.   (V.i, 291)

Outsides of course are never to be trusted:

> How many are whores in small ruffs and still looks!

but nor are reputations, either good or bad:

> How many chaste, whose names fill slander's books!
> (V.i, 318)

Sir Alexander in fact is as incapable of identifying an honest man (or woman) as Lord Noland of spotting a thief, because he has always looked with the world's eyes. He and the thoroughly unlikeable Laxton are the slaves of conventional opinion and alike believe without question that everyone can be bought[35]—an aspect of the con-

---

[35] 'Money is that aqua fortis that eats into many a maidenhead: where the walls are flesh and blood, I'll ever pierce through with a golden auger' (II.i, 176). Sir Alexander plays the contemptible trick of tempting Moll to steal so that she may come into his legal clutches (IV.i); but there is something nasty in the rather similar temptation which Master Openwork successfully lays for Goshawk (II.i), and even Moll makes as though to put Mistress Tiltyard's chastity to the test, though that episode, if ever it was written, was cancelled from the final copy. (See II.i, 311.)

ventional view that all are motivated solely by self-interest: Curtilax
the sergeant has doubtless seen enough of villainy to justify in his
eyes the generalization that 'all that live in the world are but great
fish and little fish, and feed upon one another' (III.iii, 135). But it
isn't true that everyone has his price: it is their moral blindness
which puts both Laxton and Sir Alexander in Moll's power.
Paradoxically she, about whom everyone in the play is so unsure,
is the one who never pretends to be what she is not; and this
despite her momentarily cloaking herself in front of Laxton, and
her parts as music-master and false bride. Her honesty gives her
the right as well as the power to be outspoken as well as fearless—
in speech and action. Her male clothes are thus not a disguise but
an expression of her masculine vigour and toughness; in the
scene (III.i) in which she challenges Laxton, she must be dressed as
a man to fight with him (he finds in the impossibility of drawing on a
woman a ready excuse for his own cowardice). The complex
deception in IV.i makes a different point. Moll's essential honesty
enables her to avoid Sir Alexander's snares without difficulty, but
the hastily contrived music-master plot doesn't deceive him as Moll
and Sebastian believe (see IV.i, 153–206). Yet at the really important
level for them all, this confirms his deception, for Moll is only there
to conceal Sebastian's relations with Mary: the failure to persuade
Sir Alexander that Moll is anything but who she is hides Mary's
presence from him altogether.

Moll's passage of arms and words with Laxton is the pivot of the
play, even though it is a relatively isolated episode. For she is the
moral centre freely judging others in language which is frequently
brusque, and offering, especially in this scene, the standards against
which all actions and intentions are to be judged. Opinions of her
from commentators tend to be picturesque. To Bullen she is

> the Amazon of Bankside . . . She moves among rowdies and pro-
> fligates without suffering any contamination; she has the thews
> of a giant and the gentleness of a child. Secure in her 'armed and
> iron maidenhood', and defying the breath of scandal, she daffs the
> world aside and chooses a life of frolic freedom.[36]

Eliot more solemnly finds her 'a type of the sort of woman who has
renounced all happiness for herself and who lives only for principle',
a realization of 'a free and noble womanhood'.[37] The renunciation
of happiness sounds like a reference to the riddling verses she speaks
in the last scene to explain her not having married:

[36] op. cit., I, xxxv. The thews indeed but not the sinews—not to recognize
which is the fault of the detractors who accuse her of bisexualism.
[37] *Selected Essays*, 167, 170.

> When you shall hear
> Gallants void from sergeants' fear,
> Honesty and truth unslandered,
> Woman manned but never pandered,
> Cheators booted but not coached,
> Vessels older ere they're broached.
> If my mind be then not varied,
> Next day following I'll be married.   (V.ii, 217–24)

To Lord Noland's remark, 'This sounds like doomsday', she returns
a teasing dismissal—

> Then were marriage best,
> For if I should repent, I were soon at rest

—which appears to lend some support to Miss Bradbrook's view that
by the end of the play 'the accent is no longer quite so noble, or her
character quite so unequivocal as it was'.[38] But Moll has always
teased in this way, and the list of impossibilities to be got over before
she can marry only shows she still has work to do—work which
plainly she has enjoyed throughout the play. Though she has nothing
of the frivolity which 'frolic freedom' suggests, there is little sense
of renunciation in the zest with which she tackles the shaming of
lechery or engineers an honest marriage. And while zest and energy
sometimes appear as quick temper, it is they which give credibility to
her enthusiasm for virtue. It is obviously fun to put down the
disgusting Laxton and prove him such a coward that he must end by
begging her to spare his life. But this in no way lessens the depth and
seriousness of her great speech of reproach: when Laxton, scared
and startled by her drawing a sword on him, asks 'What dost mean,
Moll?', she answers with the superb scorn of one confident of her own
power and the rightness of her cause:

> To teach thy base thoughts manners: th'art one of those
> That thinks each woman thy fond flexible whore:
> If she but cast a liberal eye upon thee,
> Turn back her head, she's thine: or, amongst company,
> By chance drink first to thee, then she's quite gone,
> There's no means to help her . . .
> How many of our sex, by such as thou
> Have their good thoughts paid with a blasted name
> That never deserved loosely or did trip
> In path of whoredom beyond cup and lip?
> But for the stain of conscience and of soul,

[38] Bradbrook, op. cit., 163. I think it a pity—and inconsistent with all we
have seen of her—that in the last scene Moll should be twice made to draw
attention to her part in the intrigue which brought about the happy finale
(V.ii, 169, 206).

> Better had women fall into the hands
> Of an act silent than a bragging nothing,
> There's no mercy in't.—What durst move you, sir,
> To think me whorish?—a name which I'd tear out
> From the high German's throat if it lay ledger there
> To despatch privy slanders against me.
> In thee I defy all men . . .   (III.i, 70)[39]

Though the situation is obviously less tense, the tone of this bears a striking affinity to Bianca's horrified speech after her betrayal in Act II, scene ii of *Women Beware Women*. But Middleton finds it in other comedy as well; and coming on the deadly seriousness with which Whorehound upbraids Allwit near the end of *A Chaste Maid*, R. B. Parker writes of Middleton's unease in the world of the city comedies 'which finally develops into the dreadful world of *Women Beware Women*'.[40] Moll is one of the few figures in Middleton to ride through this world unharmed, and it is on the strength of this that she condemns Laxton and his like in the name of all women. There is no repentance in Moll (in this she is unlike Bellafront in *The Honest Whore* and the inversion of Bianca), because there was for her no fall into the sink of debauchery which, we are to know, lies all about us from our infancy.

Moll has a special advantage for a dramatist of Middleton's turn in her ability to move classlessly at ease among people in all ranks of society: she knows the ways of thieves but is on familiar terms with a lord, even if he is one whose name suggests that, like Laxton's, all his lands are sold. There are four easily recognizable groups within the play, each more or less distinct and homogeneous, though comings and goings are frequent, and all are characterized by a busy determination to get ahead without much scruple over the means. The first group—the elderly knighted merchant aristocracy of London—are indeed already established in the pride of riches, and their aim is to keep what they have. They are the familiar stock of close-fisted age against which flush youth traditionally revolts, wagging their heads at the evil of the times but ready enough to corrupt justice for their own ends. Sir Alexander indeed is made occasionally to show signs of compunction (as when he momentarily sees how he wrongs Moll in IV.i, but conventional assumptions quickly get the better of him again) and even of a concern with last things:

---

[39] Note that here, and here alone, Moll moves from her habitual more distant mode of address to an obviously scornful second person singular (which others—too familiarly—commonly use to her), but alternates with the formal mode for power of attack.

[40] Parker, art. cit., 185.

I am old, my son,
Oh let me prevail quickly,
For I have weightier business of mine own
Than to chide thee: I must not to my grave
As a drunkard to his bed, whereon he lies
Only to sleep, and never cares to rise. (II.ii, 121)

For a moment of curious pathos we feel that he really convinces himself that he is worried about his soul till Sebastian's talk of marriage to Moll brings back the familiar bluster of self-pitying threats. It is something, doubtless, to a man of his character, that he must be brought at the end so far to humble himself as to apologize to Moll and admit the folly of looking on her with the world's eyes rather than freely with his own; yet in the general rejoicings, such self-abasement may come tolerably easily: Sir Alexander is in the end 'so far sorry' for what he has done that he will multiply sixfold the corrupt coins by which he has tried to trap Moll.

Of the gallants, who appear as sycophants to the rich old men in the first act, little more need be said. They are of a decidedly meaner cast than the cheerful tricksters of Middleton's earlier plays— Laxton in particular who merely toys with Mistress Gallipot in order to swindle her, but shows no spirit of his own; Goshawk is as bad with his 'gift of treachery to betray my friend' when he is most trustful. Jack Dapper, on the other hand, is a rare example in Middleton or Dekker of the fool simple, a bland prototype of the more sinister Ward in *Women Beware Women*.

The citizens, again, who make up the third group, rather stand apart from others of their kind in contemporary comedy, though they are cousins of those in the two *Ho!* plays. Worldly success has made them genial, and so they recall perhaps Simon Eyre in *The Shoemakers' Holiday* (though without his exuberance) rather than voracious graspers like Quomodo or Yellowhammer, or the amazing patience of the self-denying Candido in *The Honest Whore*. They are still content to serve in their shops, and it is not quite true of them, as Kathleen Lynch says of Middleton's tradesmen in general, that they 'seek for themselves the privileges and immunities enjoyed by gentlemen';[41] but Gallipot is a rich man who owns a ship, engages in trade on scale enough to have a factor, and can easily afford to rebuild his barns at Hockley Hole if they have been burnt down. He and his friends are becoming part of the City aristocracy, replacing the landed gentry by engrossing the land itself. Nevertheless, they seem at the moment to stay apart (their entry at the end is merely formal), and the men at least retain their virtue: unlike the citizens in

[41] Kathleen M. Lynch, *The Social Mode of Restoration Comedy* (New York, 1926), 28.

Westward Ho!, these do not frequent bawdy houses, and Openwork does not keep a whore in the suburbs. It is their wives who are more lecherously given, though Mistress Gallipot could be forgiven for finding her fussy and uxorious husband tiresome. In the end, of course, the wives realize how much more solidly worthwhile their husbands are than the gallants whom they can, it seems, trap so easily—though the innuendoes in the conversation between Mistress Gallipot and Mistress Openwork (IV.ii, 40ff.) are so broad that one cannot believe they have altogether given up the search for new delights. This scene is one of the few instances in the play where the joint authorship appears to have left some rough edges (see below, p. xxxiii); Holmes suggests that it was necessary to bring the citizen plots to a hasty conclusion to make way for the long canting scene before the denouement of the main action.[42]

The canting scene is an almost complete irrelevance to the remainder of the play, though it does give further evidence of Moll's prowess and the knowledge of the underworld which has given rise to her reputation and soubriquet. Trapdoor's recent induction into this world gives the (rather weak) excuse for the lengthy display of thieves' slang which is little more than a dramatized version of a canting dictionary (see Appendix, p. 146). But there is a good deal of fun to be had from it, and it completes Moll's or her authors' anatomy of knavery by bringing to the forefront the professional sharpers who had previously only passed quickly across the stage.

It also brings forward the delight in athletic verbal humour which is such a feature of *The Roaring Girl*, and of course of Middleton's other comedies. Middleton, as Christopher Ricks has remarked, was a master of innuendo, especially sexual innuendo.[43] In *The Roaring Girl* the punning and wordplay are so constant and intricate that it is often as if two conversations are going on simultaneously using the same words. Such exchanges as those between Laxton and Sir Alexander (I.ii, 55ff.) or Laxton and Goshawk (II.i, 10ff.), or Moll's conversation with her tailor (II.ii, 79ff.) and her discussion with Sebastian of the right uses of a gentleman's instrument (IV.i, 85ff.) are extended pieces of bawdry in which the scarcely concealed sexual dialogue sits on top of a perfectly consistent conversation about something quite innocent. The eye of anyone reading Middleton quickly learns to hawk for venery, and these plays offer striking evidence of the sharpness of the Elizabethan ear for innuendo and double meaning. On occasion the language has a labyrinthine brilliance which rivals Shakespeare's and seems to owe

[42] Holmes, op. cit., 109.
[43] See 'The Moral and Poetic Structure of *The Changeling*', *E in C*, X (July 1960), 291.

something to him: see Mistress Openwork's complaint at II.i, 204, which I am far from sure of having fully explored.[44]

Language of this sportive kind appears in scenes of all kinds—the innocent Mary is offered some by Neatfoot in the first lines of the play, though the hints mean nothing to her—but it is only one of a quite rich range of languages, turning naturally to popular saws and aphorisms and running from the thieves' cant (really a kind of code intended to darken the counsels of the uninitiated) to the bold clarity which Moll's fearless moral passion demands. There is an entertaining moment of another kind of (Middletonian?) verbal irony when Mistress Gallipot, spinning her yarn about Laxton to fool her ingenuous husband, tries on some poetry (which she borrows from Dekker's *Whore of Babylon*):

> Since last I saw him, twelve months three times told
> The moon hath drawn through her light silver bow.
>
> (III.ii, 120)

The effect of this from the decidedly unpoetical Mistress Gallipot is ludicrous: it takes its place in her (successful) attempt at deceiving the husband she thinks beneath her; and the involved punning and double-talk throughout the play always has a function of this kind. In the web of fraud and dissimulation through which Moll cuts her way, language is readily turned into a chief artifice of deceit.

The Roaring Girl stands out from its contemporary scene in truth on one account only—the portrait of Moll. In other respects, supple, energetic, and ingenious as it is, the play is a middling example of its highly enjoyable kind. It shows a skill in the manipulation of language which at times reaches brilliance and is always capable of yielding much pleasure, though, unlike Shakespeare's or Jonson's, not often capable of making or leading to depth of understanding or discovery: the linguistic jugglery is really too much of the surface for that; and the organization of the several plots is a good deal more elementary, less interesting and entertaining in itself, than in the two or three best comedies which Middleton wrote on his own. The play is less completely taken up with the making of money than, say, *Michaelmas Term* or *A Trick to Catch the Old One*, but displays to the full and openly the Jacobean obsession with sex. That, like everything else in *The Roaring Girl*, Moll knows about, understands, and has learnt or taught herself to judge. It is the combination of high spirits and quick thinking with her determination to act her own part in keeping up virtue and tracking down vice, which makes her so attractive and unusual a figure in the drama of

[44] It has scarcely seemed necessary in the notes to set out all the obscene punning in explicit detail, but very likely I have missed some altogether.

her time or indeed any other: she has the spirit of one who has seen the world enough to undervalue it with good breeding, of one whose virtue sits easily about her and to whom vice is thoroughly contemptible. The great delight for the reader—and perhaps sometime for an audience—is that her vivacious scorn of evil finds its natural expression in the tough, athletic rhythms of her own lines and so irresistibly compels itself on those who hear:

> she that has wit and spirit
> May scorn
> To live beholding to her body for meat,
> Or for apparel, like your common dame
> That makes shame get her clothes to cover shame.
> Base is that mind that kneels unto her body,
> As if a husband stood in awe on's wife;
> My spirit shall be mistress of this house,
> As long as I have time in't.   (III.i, 132)

THE SHARES OF THE TWO AUTHORS

The title-page of the quarto tells us that *The Roaring Girl* was 'written by Thomas Middleton and Thomas Dekker'; and Middleton's name also appears at the foot of the Epistle to the Readers. Beyond that there is no documentary evidence of the two writers' shares, and opinions have varied from one extreme to the other. On the one hand Fleay[45] thought that Middleton wrote only three scenes (II.ii, IV.i, and V.ii), and Alfred Harbage perhaps leans to this view, for he writes[46] of Dekker's having 'let Middleton sign the preface'. Bowers certainly does, though without giving reasons beyond saying that the hypothesis that Dekker prepared the fair copy from which the printers worked 'helps to explain a scene or two in which the authorship seems somewhat mixed'.[47] At the other extreme Holmes[48] writes of Middleton as having 'obtained Dekker's assistance for a special scene in *The Roaring Girl*' (i.e., V.i), though it appears from his detailed discussion of the play that he does not quite limit Dekker's contribution to this scene alone. Others have divided the play in various ways, their opinions being conveniently tabulated in the article by G. R. Price, which is the only comprehensive attempt at a critical and linguistic analysis of this problem.[49]

[45] *Biographical Chronicle of the English Drama*, I, 132.
[46] 'The Mystery of *Perkin Warbeck*', in Bennett, Cargill, and Hall, eds, *Studies in the English Renaissance Drama* (1961), 129.
[47] Bowers, III, 8.
[48] Holmes, op. cit., xviii.
[49] Price (Shares), 614.

∙ ∙

The Roaring Girl certainly stands away from the line of London comedies which Middleton wrote unaided on either side of it, though its distinguishing characteristics are not necessarily all to be attributed to Dekker's presence. That the play is by and large more ingratiating and warm-hearted than *Michaelmas Term* or *A Trick to Catch the Old One* certainly suggests Dekker's relaxing, sentimental hand, and the overall tone recalls that of *The Honest Whore*. With the exception of Laxton's self-induced eclipse by Moll in III.i, all the denouements take a comparatively cosy turn quite unlike the ironic rewards reaped by Middleton's rogues: the sour old men and the gallants (who likewise have little humour to them) are exposed and corrected in scenes where the sentiment is commonplace: especially is this true of IV.ii, which is in marked contrast with the previous citizen scenes (II.i and III.ii), where the dialogue has the smartness and rapidity and the situations the ingenious irony characteristic of Middleton; in this closing citizen scene, on the other hand, we are shown, in Price's words, 'instead of ironic satire . . . an unimpressive pseudo-morality converting Mistress Gallipot and Openwork to rectitude and the delightfully foolish Master Galli pot into a surly wronged husband who finally invites his enemy to dinner'.[50]

Price observes that

the play is decidedly Middletonian in that, despite the romantic love plot which brings Moll Cutpurse most into the action, episodic realistic intrigue makes up not only all of the shopkeeper's subplot, but a large part of the main plot. Contrasting a romance with an action of cynical and realistic humor is characteristic of Middleton.

It is not unknown in Dekker either, or at least it appears in other plays in which he collaborated. It is perhaps true, as Price says, that 'the plan of construction [reveals] . . . more effort to attain unity than Dekker usually made',[51] but this is nothing to go on, especially since such unity as it achieves is only clumsily maintained by the tenuous links via the gallants; for Moll is absent from the citizen plots, and even her presence cannot conceal the dramatic inconsequence of the long canting scene, which appears like a vaudeville interlude: this scene is the only one on whose authorship everyone agrees, for it shows a delight in playing with foreign languages (especially Dutch) which is peculiarly Dekker's, and the thieves' cant, which had at least an equal fascination for him, follows closely the usage set out in the almost exactly contemporary *Bellman of*

[50] Price (Shares), 611f.
[51] Price (Shares), 606, 613.

London and *Lanthorn and Candlelight*.[52] The constructional clumsiness of the play—so different from the tight mesh of plots in Middleton's best comedies—probably indicates nothing beyond a certain lack of concentration and the inevitable difficulties of collaboration. It is not easy to see where the joins are; but the seamless unity on which Miss Bradbrook congratulates Middleton does allow for a good deal of looseness within.

What is more characteristically his is, as Holmes rightly insists,

> a remarkable didactic force . . . running through the very texture of the play . . . The pervasiveness of that didactic force shows, more clearly than any other feature, that whichever of the authors did more of the actual writing, the development of the whole was under Middleton's direction.[53]

What in this context needs a little more stress is the extent to which this didactic force is embodied in Moll. A. W. Ward[54] notes that 'the bright vivacity which gives something like a charm to this strange figure may be confidently ascribed to Middleton; but the character of her charm is that of a moral energy and enthusiasm which, unique as she is, are specially Middletonian'. Middleton shows a deeper interest in portraying women than any of his contemporaries except Shakespeare, and a more constant interest even than his. Moll *is* the moral force of the play (the sentimental reproofs of Openwork and Gallipot are by contrast mechanical and conventional stuff), and her passionate energy is akin to that which, though it does not motivate them as characters, invests the portraits of Beatrice and Bianca in Middleton's two great tragedies. One has only to think of a characteristic Dekker heroine such as Jane in *The Shoemakers' Holiday* or the conventionally upright wives in *Westward Ho!* and *Northward Ho!* to see how far beyond Dekker's range are Moll's 'intellectual and moral originality'. The phrase is William Power's, who remarks[55] that 'her ability to call social and moral values into question, particularly those which subject woman to man, suggests a character from Ibsen or Shaw'. Perhaps an occasional gentleness in her may be due to Dekker, but the prime conception and working-out of the character are Middleton's. (On the other hand, Power's argument that the duplication of the name

---

[52] Price (Shares, 612) believes that this scene fits so awkwardly into the rest of the play that 'it is either an expansion of an episode or two which proved such a hit in the theater that Dekker rewrote them at length, or a scene Dekker had written before the rest of the play was composed or conceived'.

[53] Holmes, op. cit., 100f.

[54] *History of English Dramatic Literature*, 2nd edn (1899), II, 519, quoted by Holmes, loc. cit.

[55] 'Double, Double', *N & Q*, VI, 1 (Jan. 1959), 5.

Mary indicates that Dekker was *independently* responsible for most of the main plot is surely unacceptable. Mary Frith's name was well known, and Dekker cannot have *accidentally* given the name to Mary Fitz-Allard as well. Moll after all is Mary's stand-in in different ways in both parts of Sebastian's stratagem, and the identity of name is used deliberately: cf., for example, the implications of the dialogue in II.ii, 143–76.)

Price's linguistic analysis of the verse of the play confirms the view that Middleton wrote the larger part: he assigns to Dekker alone only three scenes (III.iii, IV.ii, and V.i, with Middleton's hand visible as reviser in the first of these), all the rest to Middleton except for the opening act worked out together. The fact that there has been so much argument about the two men's shares is in any case some evidence of the closeness with which they collaborated. But the character and power of the central figure and all that she represents show the controlling hand to be Middleton's.

A NOTE ON THE TEXT

The Roaring Girl was published by Thomas Archer in 1611 in the only early edition known; Archer did not enter it in the Stationers' Register.[56] Ten copies of the first quarto are known to have survived and are listed in Bowers's textual edition of the play.[57] The present text was prepared from a photographic reproduction of that in the Dyce Collection at the Victoria and Albert Museum, collated with one of two copies in the British Museum (Ashley 1159) and one in the Bodleian Library (Malone 246[1]). I have also used the text prepared by Professor Bowers, which notes all press-variants within the available copies of the quarto, as well as others noted below.

Most of these variants represent the correction of literals and minor amendments of punctuation which are of no significance. Substantive changes occur only in signature I (1^v and $4^{r \& v}$), i.e., IV.ii, 49ff. and 221ff. The second of these involved resetting of type loosened when a forme was unlocked for a correction, but no verbal variants; those which occur in the first have no authority. A summary of the evidence of proof-correction is given in the textual introduction to Bowers's edition, which should be consulted for detailed information on variant-readings and accidentals, few of which are recorded in the notes to the present edition. All the few major cruces in the play are discussed briefly in the notes; the only one worth mentioning here is that which was responsible for the alterations at IV.ii, 49 and 53. All copies of Q agree in having two consecutive speeches with the same prefix, the second occurrence of which is as the catchword at the bottom of a page. An attempt was apparently made during printing to correct this anomaly, but abandoned, though not without alterations working their way in.

The quarto was evidently printed from a carefully prepared manuscript, which Bowers and Price[58] believe to be Dekker's work, though it contains a number of contractions characteristic of Middleton. The transcription was either a fair copy made for the actors or derived from the prompt book—as might be suggested by the comprehensive but somewhat inconsistently worded and occasionally misaligned stage directions. Punctuation is variable and occasionally capricious, though generally—as in most of Middleton—

[56] Bald's view (Chronology, 37) that the 'book concerninge Mall Cutpurse' entered in *S.R.* by Ambrose Garland on 18 February 1612 may be *The Roaring Girl* is really guesswork.

[57] See Bowers, III, 9, and Greg, 298.

[58] Price (Manuscript and Quarto), 182–3.

light, with extensive use of commas where we might use heavier stops, which were indeed liberally provided by nineteenth-century editors. I have tried to preserve this lightness which seems appropriate for the racy conversational idiom in which so much of the play is written, while bringing some consistency to such matters as capitalization and the use of question-marks (commonly omitted from Q, and where present often anticipating the end of the sentence). Some order has likewise been brought into common constructions which have, like the spelling, all been modernized, so that we read 'I'm' for 'Ime' or 'I'me', 'I'll' for 'Ile', 'You'd' for 'Youlde' and so on. I have kept 'Y'are' where it appears in the copy-text, for it implies a different pronunciation from 'You're', which in this edition where necessary replaces 'Your'. I have also made some attempt to relineate a few passages in which what seemed to me manifestly verse is printed as prose or, occasionally, vice versa. This is a task which must be approached with great caution, for Middleton's verse in particular is highly irregular, containing many lines of greater or less than normal length. Moreover, he moves easily from verse to a strongly rhythmical prose, and some passages are in a mixture of the two: any attempt at wholesale regularization of the verse is therefore to be avoided; nevertheless, it is clear that some of the irregularities are the result of compositorial endeavours to save or lose space, and these it is misplaced piety to retain. Asides are frequent, though rarely noted as such in Q: I have identified them where it seemed possible that readers might be misled, and have also supplied a few missing stage directions. There are no act and scene divisions in Q: this edition follows those established by Dyce, except that I agree with Bowers in dividing Act I into two scenes.

Since the first quarto, *The Roaring Girl* has appeared in Dodsley's *Select Collection of Old Plays* (1780), in Sir Walter Scott's *Ancient British Drama* (1810), vol. II, and, edited by J. P. Collier, in the third edition of Dodsley (1825). It was included in vol. II of Dyce's *Works of Thomas Middleton* (1840), the first to establish a canon. Bullen's edition of the *Works* (1885), in which *The Roaring Girl* appears in vol. IV, is based closely on Dyce; and Havelock Ellis's selection in the old Mermaid series (1887: *Roaring Girl* in vol. II) is virtually a reprint of parts of Bullen. A facsimile of one of the British Museum copies was issued by J. S. Farmer for the Tudor Facsimile Texts (1914). Its most recent appearance is the full textual edition of Fredson Bowers in vol. III of *The Dramatic Works of Thomas Dekker* (1958).

FURTHER READING

Anon, *The Life and Death of Mrs Mary Frith, commonly called Mall Cutpurse*, 1662.

Bald, R. C., 'The Sources of Middleton's City Comedies', *Journal of English and Germanic Philology*, XXXIII (1934), 373–87.

Bald, R. C., 'The Chronology of Middleton's Plays', *MLR*, XXXII (1937), 33–43.

Barker, R. H., *Thomas Middleton*, New York, 1958.

Bradbrook, M. C., *The Growth and Structure of Elizabethan Comedy*, 2nd edn, 1973.

Dunkel, W. D., *The Dramatic Technique of Thomas Middleton in his Comedies of London Life*, Chicago, 1925.

Dowling, Margaret, 'A Note on Moll Cutpurse—"The Roaring Girl"', *RES*, X (1934), 67–71.

Eccles, M., 'Middleton's Birth and Education', *RES*, VII (1931), 431.

Eccles, M., 'Thomas Middleton a Poett', *SP*, LIV (1957), 516–36.

Eliot, T. S. 'Thomas Middleton', *Elizabethan Essays*, 1927; and *Selected Essays*, 2nd edn, 1934.

Ellis-Fermor, Una, *The Jacobean Drama*, 4th edn 1958, repr. with extra bibliography, 1961.

Farr, Dorothy M., *Thomas Middleton and the Drama of Realism*, Edinburgh, 1973.

Gibbons, Brian, *Jacobean City Comedy*, 1968.

Holmes, David M., *The Art of Thomas Middleton*, Oxford, 1970.

Knights, L. C., *Drama and Society in the Age of Jonson*, 1937.

Lynch, Kathleen M., *The Social Mode of Restoration Comedy*, New York, 1926.

Parker, R. B., 'Middleton's Experiments with Comedy and Judgment' in Brown and Harris, eds, *Stratford-upon-Avon Studies*, I: *Jacobean Theatre* (1960), 179-200.

Power, William, 'Double, Double', *N & Q*, VI (1959), 4–8.

Price, George R., 'The Shares of Middleton and Dekker in a Collaborated Play', *Papers from the Michigan Academy of Arts and Sciences*, XXX (1945), 601–15.

Price, George R., 'The Manuscript and Quarto of *The Roaring Girl*', *The Library* (Fifth series), XI (1956), 182–3.

Ricks, Christopher, 'The Moral and Poetic Structure of *The Changeling*', *E in C*, X (1960), 290–306.

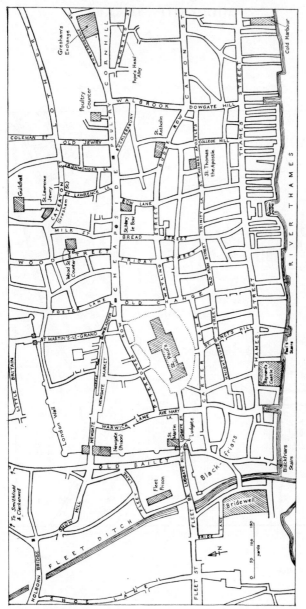

Central London in the early seventeenth century

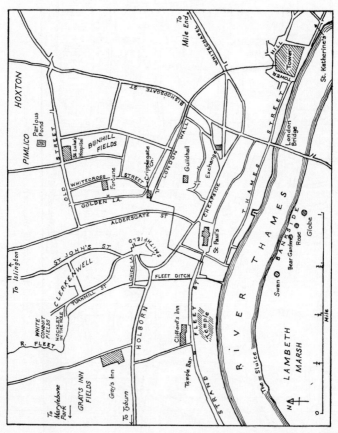

London and the northern suburbs

The Roaring Girle.

OR
Moll Cut-Purse.

As it hath lately beene Acted on the Fortune-stage by
the Prince his Players.

Written by *T. Middleton* and *T. Dekkar.*

My case is alter'd, I must worke for my liuing.

Printed at *London* for *Thomas Archer*, and are to be sold at his
shop in Popes head-pallace, neere the Royall
Exchange. 1611.

The Fortune-stage The Fortune Theatre was built, on a site in Golden Lane, Cripplegate, in 1600. It was a large building (cf. Prologus, 10), 80 feet square outside, 53 inside, with three tiers of galleries: a reconstruction by W. H. Godfrey, based on the still surviving contract, is given on p. xviii. I have preferred Godfrey's reconstruction to that of Mr C. Walter Hodges (*The Globe Restored*, 1953, p. 175), which seems to me in its general cast too baroque and is in some constructional detail certainly at fault. As Hodges has shown, however, the supporting structure of the stage should have visible pilasters along the front. The theatre was burnt down in 1621, rebuilt two years later in circular form, and finally destroyed in 1661. It is frequently mentioned in contemporary plays and other writings.

The Prince his Players In 1603 the Admiral's Men, who had for over twenty years been the servants of Lord Howard of Effingham, Lord High Admiral, were transferred to Prince Henry, James I's eldest son. Three years before, they had made the Fortune their permanent home under the lucrative but somewhat tyrannical overlordship of Edward Alleyn and Philip Henslowe, whose diary (up to 1603) provides copious notes of the company's activities.

Popes head-pallace The Pope's Head Tavern in Pope's Head Alley (a lane running south from Cornhill to Lombard Street) may have been originally part of King John's palace. More than one bookseller is recorded as issuing books from the 'Palace', and the alley was largely occupied by booksellers' shops from about 1600. Thomas Archer was also the printer in 1609 of the anonymous *Every Woman in Her Humour*.

My case is alter'd, I must worke for my liuing The first half of the sentence is a common proverbial expression, giving title to one of Jonson's comedies (1597 published 1609). The whole sentence may be a quotation: it bears obviously on the main theme of *A Chaste Maid in Cheapside*, but its relevance to *The Roaring Girl* isn't apparent.

Moll (i.e. Mary Frith) is shown in the picture wearing 'the great Dutch, slop' (see II.ii, 79); she has a 'standing collar' (III.iii 26) and 'roses' on her shoes (IV.ii, 7).

TO THE COMIC PLAY-READERS,
VENERY AND LAUGHTER

The fashion of play-making I can properly compare to nothing
so naturally as the alteration in apparel: for in the time of the
great crop-doublet, your huge bombasted plays, quilted with
mighty words to lean purpose, was only then in fashion. And as
the doublet fell, neater inventions began to set up. Now in the   5
time of spruceness, our plays follow the niceness of our gar-
ments, single plots, quaint conceits, lecherous jests, dressed up
in hanging sleeves, and those are fit for the times and the
termers: such a kind of light-colour summer stuff, mingled
with diverse colours, you shall find this published comedy,   10
good to keep you in an afternoon from dice, at home in your
chambers; and for venery you shall find enough for sixpence,
but well couched and you mark it. For Venus being a woman
passes through the play in doublet and breeches, a brave disguise and a safe one, if the statute untie not her codpiece point.   15

---

8 *hanging sleeves* no longer caught in at the cuff
9 *termers* those who came to London for the terms of the inns of
    court, often just for amusement
13 *well couched* richly embroidered, and hence not immediately
    apparent
13 *and* an, if

Title *Venery*. Good hunting, or (in this play more importantly) the pursuit
    of sexual pleasure. Cf. III.i, 40 and *Northward Ho!*, III.i, 87: 'Venery
    is like usury . . . it may be allowed though it be not lawful'.
  3 *crop-doublet*. A short doublet, richly padded, which went out of fashion
    about 1580. Stubbes in his *Anatomy of Abuses* (1583) writes of 'doublets
    with great bellies . . . stuffed with four, five, or six pounds of bombast
    at the least'. Bombast was cotton wool used for stuffing, but the word
    was regularly in figurative use as well.
4–5 *as the doublet fell*. It became longer and longer till the 1590s, but then
    shrank and became hollow-bellied.
  7 *single plots* were hardly characteristic of 1611 (or 1608), and Middleton
    may be writing ironically.
 12 *sixpence*. The ordinary price of a (printed) play.
 15 *if the statute untie not her codpiece point*. Though there was much legis-
    lation regulating the dress of particular trades and classes, none is
    known which proscribed women from wearing men's clothes. Presum-
    ably, therefore, the phrase is proleptic: 'provided no law is made to
    prevent her going dressed as a man'. Points were tags used to tie breeches
    or doublet (see III.i, 58).

3

The book I make no question but is fit for many of your companies, as well as the person itself, and may be allowed both gallery room at the playhouse, and chamber room at your lodging. Worse things I must needs confess the world has taxed her for, than has been written of her; but 'tis the excellency of a writer to leave things better than he finds 'em; though some obscene fellow (that cares not what he writes against others, yet keeps a mystical bawdy-house himself, and entertains drunkards to make use of their pockets and vent his private bottle-ale at midnight)—though such a one would have ripped up the most nasty vice that ever hell belched forth, and presented it to a modest assembly, yet we rather wish in such discoveries, where reputation lies bleeding, a slackness of truth, than a fullness of slander.

THOMAS MIDDLETON.

---

23 *mystical* secret, unavowed
25 *ripped up* brought into the open

---

18 *gallery room.* The tiring room at the Fortune was an enclosed continuation of the upper gallery; presumably copies of plays were kept here.
19 *Worse things.* For what had been written of Moll Cutpurse see above, pp. xiii–xvi.
24 *vent his private bottle-ale.* There seems almost certainly some sexual joke here, but I cannot reconstruct it. 'Bottle-ale' appears in *2 Henry IV*, II.iv, 128, where the Arden editor suggests it means small beer; and this seems to be confirmed by a remark in Nashe's *Foulweather's Prognostications* (*Works*, ed. Wilson, III, 392): 'the predominant qualities of this [the summer] quarter is heat and dryness, whereby I do gather that, through the influence of Cancer, bottle-ale shall be in great authority, and wheat shall do knights' service unto malt. Tapsters this quarter shall be in greater credit than cobblers, and many shall drink more than they can earn'. But it could also mean simply windy rhetoric (see Marston, *Histriomastix*, III.i, 202); 'vent' can mean sniff out, uncover, or emit (urine, wind, etc.), and 'bottle' was one of innumerable words for the female pudenda (cf. *Measure for Measure*, III.ii, 174).

PROLOGUS

A play expected long makes the audience look
For wonders:—that each scene should be a book,
Composed to all perfection; each one comes
And brings a play in's head with him: up he sums
What he would of a roaring girl have writ;   5
If that he finds not here, he mews at it.
Only we entreat you think our scene
Cannot speak high (the subject being but mean);
A roaring girl, whose notes till now never were,
Shall fill with laughter our vast theatre,   10
That's all which I dare promise: tragic passion,
And such grave stuff, is this day out of fashion.
I see attention sets wide ope her gates
Of hearing, and with covetous listening waits,
To know what girl this roaring girl should be.   15
For of that tribe are many: one is she
That roars at midnight in deep tavern bowls,
That beats the watch, and constables controls;
Another roars i'th' daytime, swears, stabs, gives braves,
Yet sells her soul to the lust of fools and slaves.   20
Both these are suburb-roarers. Then there's beside
A civil city-roaring girl, whose pride,
Feasting, and riding, shakes her husband's state,
And leaves him roaring through an iron grate.
None of these roaring girls is ours: she flies   25
With wings more lofty. Thus her character lies,—
Yet what need characters, when to give a guess
Is better than the person to express?
But would you know who 'tis? would you hear her name?
She is called Mad Moll; her life our acts proclaim.   30

---

6 *mews* jeers by mewing   14 *covetous* eager
18 *beats the watch* knocks the watchman about (the watch were in the
   charge of a constable)
19 *gives braves* offers battle   21 *beside* ed. (besides Q)
24 *through an iron grate* i.e., in prison

---

10 *our vast theatre.* The Fortune was a large theatre, though not excessively
   so: see note to title-page, and the illustration above, p. xviii.
21 *suburb-roarers.* Lower-class, with a dig at the proverbially licentious
   character of London suburbs. Cf. V.ii, 25 and note.

DRAMATIS PERSONAE

SIR ALEXANDER WENGRAVE, *and* NEATFOOT *his man*
SIR ADAM APPLETON
SIR DAVY DAPPER
SIR BEAUTEOUS GANYMEDE
[SIR THOMAS LONG]   5
LORD NOLAND
Young [SEBASTIAN] WENGRAVE
JACK DAPPER, *and* GULL *his page*
GOSHAWK
GREENWIT — *inexperience in trickery, fooling*   10
LAXTON

TILTYARD [*à feather-seller*] ⎫
OPENWORK [*a sempster*]   ⎬ *Cives & Uxores*
GALLIPOT [*an apothecary*]   ⎭

MOLL *the Roaring Girl* — *plays clever servant helper, ali*   15
as well as woman in own right
TRAPDOOR
[TEARCAT]

SIR GUY FITZ-ALLARD
MARY FITZ-ALLARD *his daughter*

CURTILAX *a Sergeant, and*   20
HANGER *his Yeoman*

Ministri

1, 7 WENGRAVE ed. (Wentgraue Q)
1 NEATFOOT ed. (Neats-foot Q)
13 *Cives & Uxores* citizens and their wives
22 *Ministri* servants

---

12 TILTYARD. The word means a tilting or jousting ground: its aptness for
   a feather-seller possibly lies in the link between feathers and archery,
   or feathers and gallants.
13 OPENWORK. Work made like lace or crochet to show a pattern of holes.
14 GALLIPOT. A small glazed earthenware jar, especially one used for
   medicines, and hence a jocular name for an apothecary. Cf. also *The
   Honest Whore*, part 2, I.ii, 139: 'a harlot . . . is the gallipot to which
   these drones fly'.

[*Coachman*
Porter
Tailor
Gentlemen
Cutpurses
Fellow]

THE ROARING GIRL

Act I, Scene i

Enter MARY FITZ-ALLARD *disguised like a sempster with a case for bands, and* NEATFOOT *a serving-man with her, with a napkin on his shoulder and a trencher in his hand, as from table*

NEATFOOT

The young gentleman, our young master, Sir Alexander's son, is it into his ears, sweet damsel, emblem of fragility, you desire to have a message transported, or to be transcendent?

MARY

A private word or two, sir, nothing else.

NEATFOOT

You shall fructify in that which you come for: your pleasure   5
shall be satisfied to your full contentation: I will, fairest tree of generation, watch when our young master is erected, that is to say, up, and deliver him to this your most white hand.

MARY

Thanks, sir.

NEATFOOT

And withal certify him, that I have culled out for him, now   10
his belly is replenished, a daintier bit or modicum than any lay upon his trencher at dinner. Hath he notion of your name, I beseech your chastity?

MARY

One, sir, of whom he bespake falling bands.

NEATFOOT

Falling bands, it shall so be given him.—If you please to ven-   15
ture your modesty in the hall, amongst a curl-pated company

---

s.d. *case for bands* a box for holding collar-bands
14 *falling bands* bands worn falling flat round the neck (said by Evelyn to be a new mode in 1625)

---

s.d. *sempster.* The form of the word, now restricted to the masculine, was originally, like all *-ster* forms, feminine.
 3 *transcendent.* Unless the word has an unidentified obscene meaning, Neatfoot must mean it to imply a private colloquy between Mary and Sebastian, but his language is of course deliberately affected. cf. Osric (*Hamlet*, V.ii) and, for a closer parallel, Dondolo (*Revenger's Tragedy*, II.i).
16 *curl-pated.* Curling the hair was much affected at this time: Macaulay speaks of the curl-pated minions of James I.

9

of rude serving-men, and take such as they can set before you,
you shall be most seriously, and ingeniously welcome.
MARY
I have dined indeed already, sir.
NEATFOOT
Or will you vouchsafe to kiss the lip of a cup of rich Orleans   20
in the buttery amongst our waiting-women?
MARY
Not now in truth, sir.
NEATFOOT
Our young master shall then have a feeling of your being
here: presently it shall so be given him.   *Exit* NEATFOOT
MARY
I humbly thank you, sir. But that my bosom   25
Is full of bitter sorrows, I could smile
To see this formal ape play antic tricks:
But in my breast a poisoned arrow sticks,
And smiles cannot become me. Love woven slightly
(Such as thy false heart makes) wears out as lightly,   30
But love being truly bred i'th' soul (like mine)
Bleeds even to death, at the least wound it takes:
The more we quench this fire, the less it slakes.
Oh me!

Enter SEBASTIAN WENGRAVE *with* NEATFOOT

SEBASTIAN
A sempster speak with me, sayest thou?   35
NEATFOOT
Yes sir, she's there, *viva voce*, to deliver her auricular con-
fession.
SEBASTIAN
With me, sweetheart? What is't?

18 *ingeniously* ingenuously (the two words were often confused)
19 *dined* ed. (dyed Q)
20 *Orleans* wine from the Loire area, often referred to in contemporary plays
33 *fire* ed. (Q omits)

30 *thy* (stet Q). Perhaps we should read 'the', which would confirm the
   proverbial character of Mary's observations; but she may be making a
   direct complaint of Sebastian.
36 *auricular confession.* The phrase was normally used of confession to a
   priest, and hence implied suspicion of something treasonable. 'Confession' frequently had sexual overtones.

MARY
I have brought home your bands, sir.
SEBASTIAN
Bands?—Neatfoot.   40
NEATFOOT
Sir.
SEBASTIAN
Prithee look in, for all the gentlemen are upon rising.
NEATFOOT
Yes sir, a most methodical attendance shall be given.
SEBASTIAN
And dost hear? if my father call for me, say I am busy with a
sempster.   45
NEATFOOT
Yes sir, he shall know it that you are busied with a needle-
woman.
SEBASTIAN
In's ear, good Neatfoot.
NEATFOOT
It shall be so given him.   *Exit* NEATFOOT
SEBASTIAN
Bands? y'are mistaken, sweetheart, I bespake none: when,   50
where, I prithee? what bands? let me see them.
MARY
Yes sir, a bond fast sealed, with solemn oaths,
Subscribed unto (as I thought) with your soul,
Delivered as your deed in sight of heaven:
Is this bond cancelled, have you forgot me?   55
SEBASTIAN
Ha! life of my life, Sir Guy Fitz-Allard's daughter,
What has transformed my love to this strange shape?
Stay: make all sure.—So: now speak and be brief,
Because the wolf's at door that lies in wait
To prey upon us both. Albeit mine eyes   60

---

46 *needlewoman*. A cant word for a harlot: this brings to a climax Neatfoot's
   obscene punning which I take to be so broad earlier in the scene as not
   to need special identification.
52 *bond*. 'Bond' and 'band' were used interchangeably in the figurative
   senses.
59 *the wolf's at door*. 'To keep the wolf from the door' was proverbial from
   an early date: cf. Skelton, *Colin Clout*, 146ff., 'some there be . . . Like
   Aaron and Ure,/The wolf from the door/To werrin and to keep/From
   their ghostly sheep'.

Are blessed by thine, yet this so strange disguise
Holds me with fear and wonder.
MARY   Mine's a loathed sight,
  Why from it are you banished else so long?
SEBASTIAN
  I must cut short my speech: in broken language,
  Thus much: sweet Moll, I must thy company shun,   65
  I court another Moll, my thoughts must run
  As a horse runs that's blind, round in a mill,
  Out every step, yet keeping one path still.
MARY
  Hm! must you shun my company? in one knot
  Have both our hands by th'hands of heaven been tied,   70
  Now to be broke? I thought me once your bride:
  Our fathers did agree on the time when:
  And must another bedfellow fill my room?
SEBASTIAN
  Sweet maid, let's lose no time: 'tis in heaven's book
  Set down, that I must have thee: an oath we took   75
  To keep our vows; but when the knight your father
  Was from mine parted, storms began to sit
  Upon my covetous father's brow, which fell
  From thence on me: he reckoned up what gold
  This marriage would draw from him, at which he swore,   80
  To lose so much blood could not grieve him more.
  He then dissuades me from thee, called thee not fair,
  And asked what is she but a beggar's heir?
  He scorned thy dowry of five thousand marks.
  If such a sum of money could be found,   85
  And I would match with that, he'd not undo it,
  Provided his bags might add nothing to it,
  But vowed, if I took thee, nay more, did swear it,
  Save birth, from him I nothing should inherit.
MARY
  What follows then, my shipwreck?

67 *As a horse . . . in a mill*. The horse used to turn small millstones walked
  in a constant circle round the stone; hence (in the next line), Sebastian's
  thoughts are away from their proper place, yet always keeping to the
  one path. The phrase was proverbial and used elsewhere by Dekker:
  cf. *Northward Ho!*, I.iii, 129: 'I that like a horse/Ran blindfold in a mill
  (all in one circle)'.
79 *thence* ed. (them Q). The Q reading can be defended and is retained by
  Bowers even though it seems to clash with the singular 'brow', which,
  as an alternative amendment, Dyce and Bullen correct to 'brows'.

SEBASTIAN   Dearest, no: 90
   Though wildly in a labyrinth I go,
   My end is to meet thee: with a side wind
   Must I now sail, else I no haven can find,
   But both must sink forever. There's a wench
   Called Moll, mad Moll, or merry Moll, a creature   95
   So strange in quality, a whole city takes
   Note of her name and person: all that affection
   I owe to thee, on her in counterfeit passion
   I spend to mad my father: he believes
   I doat upon this roaring girl, and grieves   100
   As it becomes a father for a son
   That could be so bewitched: yet I'll go on
   This crooked way, sigh still for her, feign dreams
   In which I'll talk only of her: these streams
   Shall, I hope, force my father to consent   105
   That here I anchor, rather than be rent
   Upon a rock so dangerous. Art thou pleased,
   Because thou seest we are waylaid, that I take
   A path that's safe, though it be far about?
MARY
   My prayers with heaven guide thee!
SEBASTIAN   Then I will on.   110
   My father is at hand, kiss and begone;
   Hours shall be watched for meetings; I must now,
   As men for fear, to a strange idol bow.
MARY
   Farewell.
SEBASTIAN   I'll guide thee forth: when next we meet,
   A story of Moll shall make our mirth more sweet.   *Exeunt*   115

[Act I, Scene ii]

Enter SIR ALEXANDER WENGRAVE, SIR DAVY DAPPER, SIR ADAM
    APPLETON, GOSHAWK, LAXTON, and GENTLEMEN

OMNES
  Thanks, good Sir Alexander, for our bounteous cheer.
SIR ALEXANDER
  Fie, fie, in giving thanks you pay too dear.
SIR DAVY
  When bounty spreads the table, faith 'twere sin,
  At going off, if thanks should not step in.
SIR ALEXANDER
  No more of thanks, no more: ay, marry sir.   5
  Th'inner room was too close, how do you like
  This parlour, gentlemen?
OMNES   Oh passing well.
SIR ADAM
  What a sweet breath the air casts here, so cool!
GOSHAWK
  I like the prospect best.
LAXTON   See how 'tis furnished.
SIR DAVY
  A very fair sweet room.
SIR ALEXANDER   Sir Davy Dapper,   10
  The furniture that doth adorn this room
  Cost many a fair grey groat ere it came here,
  But good things are most cheap, when th'are most dear.
  Nay when you look into my galleries,
  How bravely they are trimmed up, you all shall swear   15
  Y'are highly pleased to see what's set down there:
  Stories of men and women, mixed together

12 *grey groat.* The phrase is commonly an emphatic to suggest something of
   little value, but here perhaps means of silver.
13 *good things . . . dear.* A version of a popular saying recorded by Tilley
   in several forms, e.g., 'Good cheap is dear' and 'The dearer it is the
   cheaper'.
14ff. Sir Alexander's collection suggests a parody of the great collections
   which began to be made in Elizabeth's reign, and of which Lord
   Lumley's at Nonsuch Palace, Surrey, was an already famous example.
   Pictures were sometimes fixed to the wall so close together as to make a
   mosaic covering the wall entirely. The display hints at the kind of
   spectacular stage effects which were then becoming popular in masques
   and is a kind of visual diagram of the action of the play.

Fair ones with foul, like sunshine in wet weather;
Within one square a thousand heads are laid
So close that all of heads the room seems made;   20
As many faces there, filled with blithe looks,
Show like the promising titles of new books
Writ merrily, the readers being their own eyes,
Which seem to move and to give plaudities;
And here and there, whilst with obsequious ears   25
Thronged heaps do listen, a cutpurse thrusts and leers
With hawk's eyes for his prey: I need not show him,
By a hanging villainous look yourselves may know him,
The face is drawn so rarely. Then sir, below,
The very floor, as 'twere, waves to and fro,   30
And like a floating island seems to move,
Upon a sea bound in with shores above.

OMNES

These sights are excellent.

SIR ALEXANDER   I'll show you all:
Since we are met, make our parting comical.

Enter SEBASTIAN *and* M[ASTER] GREENWIT

SEBASTIAN

This gentleman, my friend, will take his leave, sir.   35

SIR ALEXANDER

Ha, take his leave, Sebastian? who?

SEBASTIAN   This gentleman.

SIR ALEXANDER

Your love, sir, has already given me some time,
And if you please to trust my age with more,
It shall pay double interest: good sir, stay.

GREENWIT

I have been too bold.

---

24 *plaudities* rounds of applause
34 *comical* happy, cheerful
34 s.d. here ed. (at i.32 Q)

---

31 *a floating island.* A *trompe-l'oeil* effect must be in mind here, intended to
   draw the audience more completely into the spectacle. Dekker picks up
   the idea again in *The Wonder of a Kingdom* (III.i, 16ff.) and takes the
   parody further: 'I'll pave my great hall with a floor of clouds,/Wherein
   shall move an artificial sun,/Reflecting round about me golden beams/
   Whose flames shall make the room seem all on fire . . .' All the devices
   are to give an image of the world turned upside down.

SIR ALEXANDER   Not so, sir. A merry day   40
  'Mongst friends being spent, is better than gold saved.
  Some wine, some wine. Where be these knaves I keep?

Enter three or four SERVING-MEN, *and* NEATFOOT

NEATFOOT
  At your worshipful elbow, sir.
SIR ALEXANDER
  You are kissing my maids, drinking, or fast asleep.
NEATFOOT
  Your worship has given it us right.
SIR ALEXANDER   You varlets, stir: 45
  Chairs, stools and cushions: prithee Sir Davy Dapper,
  Make that chair thine.
SIR DAVY   'Tis but an easy gift,
  And yet I thank you for it, sir, I'll take it.
SIR ALEXANDER
  A chair for old Sir Adam Appleton.
NEATFOOT
  A back friend to your worship.
SIR ADAM   Marry, good Neatfoot,   50
  I thank thee for it: back friends sometimes are good.
SIR ALEXANDER
  Pray make that stool your perch, good Master Goshawk.
GOSHAWK
  I stoop to your lure, sir.
SIR ALEXANDER   Son Sebastian,
  Take Master Greenwit to you.
SEBASTIAN   Sit, dear friend.
SIR ALEXANDER
  Nay Master Laxton—furnish Master Laxton   55

52 *Master* ed. (M. Q)
53 *lure* falconer's apparatus for recalling a hawk; *stoop* submit (a
    technical term)

---

40 *A merry day . . . gold saved.* This sounds proverbial, but is not recorded
    in Tilley or Whiting.
50 *back friend.* A backer (sc., in this instance, the back of a chair), but
    playing on the alternative meaning of false friend. At this period stools
    were still commoner than chairs even in fairly elegant houses.

With what he wants, a stone—a stool I would say,
A stool.
LAXTON   I had rather stand, sir.
SIR ALEXANDER   I know you had,
Good Master Laxton. So, so.
                              Exeunt [NEATFOOT *and*] SERVANTS
Now here's a mess of friends, and, gentlemen,
Because time's glass shall not be running long,   60
I'll quicken it with a pretty tale.
SIR DAVY   Good tales do well
In these bad days, where vice does so excel.
SIR ADAM
Begin, Sir Alexander.
SIR ALEXANDER   Last day I met
An aged man upon whose head was scored
A debt of just so many years as these   65
Which I owe to my grave: the man you all know.
OMNES
His name I pray you, sir.
SIR ALEXANDER   Nay, you shall pardon me:
But when he saw me, with a sigh that brake,
Or seemed to break, his heart-strings, thus he spake:
Oh my good knight, says he (and then his eyes   70
Were richer even by that which made them poor,
They had spent so many tears they had no more),
Oh sir, says he, you know it, for you ha' seen
Blessings to rain upon mine house and me:
Fortune, who slaves men, was my slave: her wheel   75
Hath spun me golden threads, for, I thank heaven,
I ne'er had but one cause to curse my stars.
I asked him then what that one cause might be.

56–8 lineation ed. (With what . . . stool/I had . . . stand sir./I
     know . . . So, so Q)
59 *mess* company eating together

---

56 *what he wants, a stone.* A weak quibble on Laxton's name (he lacks a
   stone) becomes an insulting jibe when one remembers that 'stone' was
   standard English for testicle. (cf. the assumed name Singlestone in *A
   Mad World, My Masters*, II.vi, 26, which plainly suggests eunuch.) To
   'stand' had various sexual meanings, here especially to have an erection;
   to stand to a woman is to prepare for intercourse, and a stallion is said
   to stand at stud.
58 s.d. here ed. (at 57 Q): *So, so* appears to be a gesture of dismissal to the
   servants.
60 *Because . . . long.* So that time should not hang heavy on us.

OMNES
  So, sir?
SIR ALEXANDER He paused; and as we often see
  A sea so much becalmed there can be found   80
  No wrinkle on his brow, his waves being drowned
  In their own rage: but when th'imperious winds
  Use strange invisible tyranny to shake
  Both heaven's and earth's foundation at their noise,
  The seas, swelling with wrath to part that fray,   85
  Rise up, and are more wild, more mad than they—
  Even so this good old man was by my question
  Stirred up to roughness, you might see his gall
  Flow even in's eyes: then grew he fantastical.
SIR DAVY
  Fantastical? ha, ha.
SIR ALEXANDER   Yes, and talked oddly.   90
SIR ADAM
  Pray sir, proceed,
  How did this old man end?
SIR ALEXANDER   Marry sir, thus.
  He left his wild fit to read o'er his cards:
  Yet then (though age cast snow on all his hairs)
  He joyed because, says he, the god of gold   95
  Has been to me no niggard: that disease
  Of which all old men sicken, avarice,
  Never infected me—
LAXTON
  [Aside] He means not himself, I'm sure.
SIR ALEXANDER   For like a lamp
  Fed with continual oil, I spend and throw   100
  My light to all that need it, yet have still
  Enough to serve myself: oh but, quoth he,
  Though heaven's dew fall thus on this aged tree,
  I have a son that like a wedge doth cleave

82 *winds* ed. (wind Q)
85 *part that fray* sc. that caused by the winds: grammar and syntax
   are jumbled and inconsequent in this passage
86 *they* sc. the winds
90 *talked* ed. (talk Q, talkt Dyce)
93 *read o'er his cards* (stet Q): reckon up his position; Bowers emends
   to 'cares'
104 *that* ed. (thats Q)

98–9 The aside interrupts the complete line which is spoken aloud.

My very heart-root.

SIR DAVY   Had he such a son?   105

SEBASTIAN

[*Aside*] Now I do smell a fox strongly.

SIR ALEXANDER

Let's see: no, Master Greenwit is not yet
So mellow in years as he; but as like Sebastian,
Just like my son Sebastian, such another.

SEBASTIAN

[*Aside*] How finely, like a fencer, my father fetches his by-   110
blows to hit me, but if I beat you not at your own weapon of
subtlety—

SIR ALEXANDER

This son, saith he, that should be
The column and main arch unto my house,
The crutch unto my age, becomes a whirlwind   115
Shaking the firm foundation—

SIR ADAM   'Tis some prodigal.

SEBASTIAN

[*Aside*] Well shot, old Adam Bell.

SIR ALEXANDER

No city monster neither, no prodigal,
But sparing, wary, civil, and (though wifeless)
An excellent husband, and such a traveller,   120
He has more tongues in his head than some have teeth.

SIR DAVY

I have but two in mine.

GOSHAWK

So sparing and so wary?
What then could vex his father so?

SIR ALEXANDER   Oh, a woman.

110 *by-blows* strokes from the side
117 *Adam Bell* the famous archer who figures in the ballad of *Adam
    Bell, Clym of the Clough and William of Cloudesley*

---

114 *The column and main arch unto my house.* cf. Tourneur, *The Atheist's
    Tragedy*, V.i, 78f.: 'On these two pillars [his sons] stood the stately
    frame/And architecture of my lofty house'.
121 *more tongues in his head than some have teeth.* This presumably alludes to
    Sebastian's knowledge of languages; but proverbial phrases about the
    tongue usually had another edge to them. 'Double-tongued' meant
    deceitful (see II.ii, 10n.); and cf. 'The tongue walks where the teeth
    speed not', a proverb quoted by Dekker in *The Gull's Horn-Book*, v.

SEBASTIAN
 A flesh-fly, that can vex any man.
SIR ALEXANDER   A scurvy woman,   125
 On whom the passionate old man swore he doated:
 A creature, saith he, nature hath brought forth
 To mock the sex of woman. It is a thing
 One knows not how to name: her birth began
 Ere she was all made: 'tis woman more than man,   130
 Man more than woman, and (which to none can hap)
 The sun gives her two shadows to one shape:
 Nay more, let this strange thing walk, stand or sit,
 No blazing star draws more eyes after it.
SIR DAVY
 A monster, 'tis some monster.
SIR ALEXANDER   She's a varlet.   135
SEBASTIAN
 [*Aside*] Now is my cue to bristle.
SIR ALEXANDER
 A naughty pack.
SEBASTIAN   'Tis false.
SIR ALEXANDER   Ha, boy?
SEBASTIAN   'Tis false.
SIR ALEXANDER
 What's false? I say she's naught.
SEBASTIAN   I say that tongue
 That dares speak so, but yours, sticks in the throat
 Of a rank villain: set yourself aside—   140

---

125 *flesh-fly* literally, a fly which deposits its eggs in dead flesh
137 *naughty pack* person of low or worthless character (cf. the still
    current 'baggage')

128ff. This passage was taken over by Field into the Mall Cutpurse scene in
    Amends for Ladies (II.i, 33ff.): see above, p. xv.
132 *two shadows to one shape*. The implication is perhaps that by witchcraft
    she has stolen a shadow and so would have power over another's soul.
    The devil was normally held to cast no shadow. Possibly Sir Alexander
    also suggests that she has one shadow for a man and one for a woman.
134 *blazing star*. i.e., a meteor, held in Elizabethan cosmology to be of ill
    omen, as belonging to the sublunary world of change and decay, and
    opposed to stars which were considered to be pure, fixed, and eternal.
    cf. *The Changeling* (ed. Bawcutt, 1958), V.iii, 154–5 and n.; and below,
    III.ii, 98 and n. Bald (Chronology, 38) suggests that the comparison
    may have been prompted by the presence of Halley's comet (see above
    p. xix).

SIR ALEXANDER
  So sir, what then?
SEBASTIAN　　　　　Any here else had lied.
  (*Aside*) I think I shall fit you.
SIR ALEXANDER
  Lie?
SEBASTIAN Yes.
SIR DAVY　　　Doth this concern him?
SIR ALEXANDER　　　　　　　[*Aside*] Ah sirrah boy,
  Is your blood heated? boils it? are you stung?
  I'll pierce you deeper yet.—Oh my dear friends,　　145
  I am that wretched father, this that son,
  That sees his ruin, yet headlong on doth run.
SIR ADAM
  Will you love such a poison?
SIR DAVY　　　　　　Fie, fie.
SEBASTIAN　　　　　　　　Y'are all mad.
SIR ALEXANDER
  Th'art sick at heart, yet feel'st it not: of all these,
  What gentleman but thou, knowing his disease　　150
  Mortal, would shun the cure? Oh Master Greenwit,
  Would you to such an idol bow?
GREENWIT　　　　　　Not I, sir.
SIR ALEXANDER
  Here's Master Laxton, has he mind to a woman
  As thou hast?
LAXTON　　　No, not I, sir.
SIR ALEXANDER　　　　　Sir, I know it.
LAXTON
  Their good parts are so rare, their bad so common,　　155
  I will have nought to do with any woman.
SIR DAVY
  'Tis well done, Master Laxton.
SIR ALEXANDER　　　　　　Oh thou cruel boy,
  Thou would'st with lust an old man's life destroy;
  Because thou see'st I'm half-way in my grave,
  Thou shovel'st dust upon me: would thou might'st have　　160
  Thy wish, most wicked, most unnatural!

142 s.d. (*Aside*) This stands in Q in roman type at the end of the line
    after a dash, evidently influenced by the spoken word 'aside' two
    lines above
142 *fit* have something ready for
155 *Their . . . their* ed. (there . . . there Q)

SIR DAVY
  Why sir, 'tis thought Sir Guy Fitz-Allard's daughter
  Shall wed your son Sebastian.
SIR ALEXANDER   Sir Davy Dapper,
  I have upon my knees wooed this fond boy
  To take that virtuous maiden.
SEBASTIAN   Hark you a word, sir.   165
  You on your knees have cursed that virtuous maiden,
  And me for loving her, yet do you now
  Thus baffle me to my face? Wear not your knees
  In such entreats, give me Fitz-Allard's daughter.
SIR ALEXANDER
  I'll give thee rats-bane rather.
SEBASTIAN   Well then you know   170
  What dish I mean to feed upon.
SIR ALEXANDER
  Hark gentlemen, he swears
  To have this cutpurse drab, to spite my gall.
OMNES
  Master Sebastian—
SEBASTIAN   I am deaf to you all.
  I'm so bewitched, so bound to my desires,   175
  Tears, prayers, threats, nothing can quench out those fires
  That burn within me.   *Exit* SEBASTIAN
SIR ALEXANDER   [*Aside*] Her blood shall quench it then.
  —Lose him not, oh dissuade him, gentlemen.
SIR DAVY
  He shall be weaned, I warrant you.
SIR ALEXANDER   Before his eyes
  Lay down his shame, my grief, his miseries.   180
OMNES
  No more, no more, away.   *Exeunt all but* SIR ALEXANDER
SIR ALEXANDER   I wash a negro,
  Losing both pains and cost: but take thy flight,
  I'll be most near thee when I'm least in sight.

---

168 *baffle* hoodwink, contradict; perhaps with a secondary meaning of
    disgrace
168 *Wear* ed. (were Q)

---

176 *quench out* (stet Q): perhaps we should omit 'out', for better scansion
    and for a more exact parallel with the following line.
181 *I wash a negro.* To wash an Ethiop (or blackamoor) white is a common
    proverbial expression first recorded in late classical times (in Lucian).

Wild buck, I'll hunt thee breathless, thou shalt run on,
But I will turn thee when I'm not thought upon.   185

Enter RALPH TRAPDOOR

Now sirrah, what are you? leave your ape's tricks and speak.
TRAPDOOR
A letter from my captain to your worship.
SIR ALEXANDER
Oh, oh, now I remember, 'tis to prefer thee into my service.
TRAPDOOR
To be a shifter under your worship's nose of a clean trencher,
when there's a good bit upon't.   190
SIR ALEXANDER
Troth, honest fellow—[*Aside*] Hm—ha—let me see,
This knave shall be the axe to hew that down
At which I stumble, has a face that promiseth
Much of a villain: I will grind his wit,
And if the edge prove fine make use of it.   195
—Come hither sirrah, canst thou be secret, ha?
TRAPDOOR
As two crafty attorneys plotting the undoing of their clients.
SIR ALEXANDER
Didst never, as thou hast walked about this town,
Hear of a wench called Moll, mad merry Moll?
TRAPDOOR
Moll Cutpurse, sir?
SIR ALEXANDER   The same, dost thou know her then?   200
TRAPDOOR
As well as I know 'twill rain upon Simon and Jude's day
next: I will sift all the taverns i'th'city, and drink half-pots

---

185 *turn* deflect (a technical hunting term)
186 *ape's tricks* fantastic or extravagant bowing
193 *has* Collier reads 'h'as', which clarifies the meaning a little

---

189 *a shifter . . . upon't.* Trapdoor, posing as a trusty servant, must also be
     implying duplicity: a shifter was a cozener, who would here cunningly
     remove the 'good bit' (or morsel) from under his master's nose. A
     trencherman or trencher-friend was a parasite or toady, and there is
     probably a hint of this too.
197 The same quip appears in *Michaelmas Term*, III.i, 146.
201 *Simon and Jude's day.* 28 October, the day on which the Liveries'
     pageants turned out, was proverbially stormy: 'Simon and Jude all the
     ships on the sea home do they crowd' (see V.S. Lean, *Collectanea*
     (1902–04), I, 381).

with all the watermen o'th'Bankside, but if you will, sir, I'll
find her out.

SIR ALEXANDER

That task is easy, do't then. Hold thy hand up: 205
What's this? is't burnt?

TRAPDOOR

No sir, no, a little singed with making fireworks.

SIR ALEXANDER

There's money, spend it: that being spent, fetch more.

TRAPDOOR

Oh sir, that all the poor soldiers in England had such a leader!
For fetching, no water-spaniel is like me.   210

SIR ALEXANDER

This wench we speak of strays so from her kind
Nature repents she made her. 'Tis a mermaid
Has tolled my son to shipwreck.

TRAPDOOR

I'll cut her comb for you.

SIR ALEXANDER

I'll tell out gold for thee then: hunt her forth,   215
Cast out a line hung full of silver hooks
To catch her to thy company: deep spendings
May draw her that's most chaste to a man's bosom.

TRAPDOOR

The jingling of golden bells, and a good fool with a hobby-
horse, will draw all the whores i'th'town to dance in a morris.   220

SIR ALEXANDER

Or rather (for that's best—they say sometimes
She goes in breeches) follow her as her man.

206 *burnt* i.e., branded (as a convicted criminal's would be)

---

203 *watermen o'th'Bankside*. 'Taylor the water-poet asserts that at this time,
between Windsor and Gravesend, there were not fewer than forty
thousand watermen' (Reed, qu. Collier).

212 *a mermaid*. Mermaids were generally regarded as sinister and often
identified with the Sirens.

214 *I'll cut her comb*. An ancient proverbial phrase: cutting a cock's comb
was a usual accompaniment of gelding. So Trapdoor will destroy Moll's
masculinity.

219 *hobby-horse*. The still common children's toy was already well known
and frequently appears as part of the fool's equipment. But a hobby-
horse was also a pantomime horse which had an important place in the
morris dance: it was formed by a man inside a frame with the head and
tail of a horse (*Sh.Eng.*, II, 438). 'Morris', however, was also used loosely
of any rather wild dance, and 'hobby-horse' commonly of a wanton.

TRAPDOOR
And when her breeches are off, she shall follow me.
SIR ALEXANDER
Beat all thy brains to serve her.
TRAPDOOR
Zounds sir, as country wenches beat cream, till butter comes.   225
SIR ALEXANDER
Play thou the subtle spider, weave fine nets
To ensnare her very life.
TRAPDOOR   Her life?
SIR ALEXANDER   Yes, suck
Her heart-blood if thou canst: twist thou but cords
To catch her, I'll find law to hang her up.
TRAPDOOR
Spoke like a worshipful bencher.   230
SIR ALEXANDER
Trace all her steps: at this she-fox's den
Watch what lambs enter: let me play the shepherd
To save their throats from bleeding, and cut hers.
TRAPDOOR
This is the goll shall do't.
SIR ALEXANDER   Be firm, and gain me
Ever thine own. This done, I entertain thee: 235
How is thy name?
TRAPDOOR
My name, sir, is Ralph Trapdoor, honest Ralph.
SIR ALEXANDER
Trapdoor, be like thy name, a dangerous step
For her to venture on, but unto me—
TRAPDOOR
As fast as your sole to your boot or shoe, sir.   240
SIR ALEXANDER
Hence then, be little seen here as thou canst,
I'll still be at thine elbow.
TRAPDOOR   The trapdoor's set.
Moll, if you budge y'are gone, this me shall crown:
A roaring boy the roaring girl puts down.
SIR ALEXANDER
God-'a'-mercy, lose no time.   *Exeunt* 245

230 *bencher* magistrate   234 *goll* cant term for hand
235 *entertain thee* take thee into my service

237 *Ralph* (pronounced—and sometimes spelt—Rafe) a common name for
   servants in contemporary plays: cf. *A Mad World, My Masters*, III.i, 5.

3—TRG * *

[Act II, Scene i]

The three shops open in a rank: the first a pothecary's shop, the next a feather-shop, the third a sempster's shop: MISTRESS GALLIPOT *in the first,* MISTRESS TILTYARD *in the next,* MASTER OPENWORK *and his* WIFE *in the third. To them enters* LAXTON, GOSHAWK *and* GREENWIT

MISTRESS OPENWORK

Gentlemen, what is't you lack? what is't you buy? See fine bands and ruffs, fine lawns, fine cambrics. What is't you lack, gentlemen, what is't you buy?

LAXTON

Yonder's the shop.

GOSHAWK

Is that she?   5

LAXTON

Peace.

GREENWIT

She that minces tobacco?

LAXTON

Ay: she's a gentlewoman born, I can tell you, though it be her hard fortune now to shred Indian pot-herbs.

GOSHAWK

Oh sir, 'tis many a good woman's fortune, when her   10
husband turns bankrupt, to begin with pipes and set up again.

LAXTON

And indeed the raising of the woman is the lifting up of the man's head at all times: if one flourish, t'other will bud as fast, I warrant ye.   15

---

s.d. *in a rank* in a row, side by side

1 *what is't you lack?* The standard street-cry of pedlars, shopmen, apprentices, etc., calling for custom.

7 *minces tobacco.* This may be a nonce use of 'minces'; tobacco was commonly sold by apothecaries.

9 *Indian pot-herbs.* Pot-herbs are simply herbs boiled in a pot; perhaps a misunderstanding of how tobacco is prepared.

11 *pipes.* Tobacco was good business (cf. III.iii, 65n.); but *pipe* is plainly used here as a cant word for penis (cf. below, 45), as at *Romeo and Juliet*, IV.v, 96.

GOSHAWK

Come, th'art familiarly acquainted there, I grope that.

LAXTON

And you grope no better i'th'dark, you may chance lie
i'th'ditch when y'are drunk.

GOSHAWK

Go, th'art a mystical lecher.

LAXTON

I will not deny but my credit may take up an ounce of pure   20
smoke.

GOSHAWK

May take up an ell of pure smock. Away, go. [*Aside*] 'Tis the
closest striker. Life, I think he commits venery forty foot
deep, no man's aware on't. I, like a palpable smockster, go to
work so openly with the tricks of art, that I'm as apparently   25
seen as a naked boy in a vial, and were it not for a gift of
treachery that I have in me to betray my friend when he puts
most trust in me—mass, yonder he is, too—and by his injury
to make good my access to her, I should appear as defective
in courting as a farmer's son the first day of his feather, that 30
doth nothing at court but woo the hangings and glass
windows for a month together, and some broken waiting-
woman forever after. I find those imperfections in my venery
that, were't not for flattery and falsehood, I should want
discourse and impudence, and he that wants impudence   35
among women is worthy to be kicked out at bed's feet.
He shall not see me yet.

16 *grope* seize, apprehend; there was a common sexual use of the
   word which here picks up Laxton's *double entendre*
19 *mystical* secret (cf. Epistle to the Comic Play-Readers, 1.23)
22 *take up an ell of pure smock* i.e., lift up a woman's under-skirt (cf.
   The Taming of the Shrew, IV.iii, 160)
23 *closest striker* most secret fornicator
30 *the first day of his feather* newly fledged
32 *broken* violated, also used of unmarried mothers

24 *smockster*. Bawd: cf. *Your Five Gallants*, V.ii, 45: 'you're a hired smockster . . . we are certified that you're a bawd'.
26 *naked boy in a vial* (i.e., phial). Steevens's suggestion—'I suppose he
   means an abortion preserved in spirits'—seems irrelevant and in-
   credible; the point is presumably the visibility of nakedness seen
   through clear glass. Naked boys is a popular name for the meadow
   saffron which flowers after its leaves have withered; but the phrase also
   occurs in *The Alchemist* (III.iv, 80–1) in such a way as to suggest cata-
   mite: 'competent means to keep himself,/His punk, and naked boy, in
   excellent fashion'.

GREENWIT

Troth this is finely shred.

LAXTON

Oh, women are the best mincers.

MISTRESS GALLIPOT

'T had been a good phrase for a cook's wife, sir.   40

LAXTON

But 'twill serve generally, like the front of a new almanac,
as thus: calculated for the meridian of cook's wives, but
generally for all Englishwomen.

MISTRESS GALLIPOT

Nay, you shall ha't, sir, I have filled it for you.

She puts it to the fire

LAXTON

The pipe's in a good hand, and I wish mine always so.   45

GREENWIT

But not to be used o'that fashion.

LAXTON

Oh pardon me, sir, I understand no French. I pray be
covered. Jack, a pipe of rich smoke.

GOSHAWK

Rich smoke? that's sixpence a pipe, is't?

GREENWIT

To me, sweet lady.   50

MISTRESS GALLIPOT

[*Aside to* LAXTON] Be not forgetful; respect my credit, seem
strange: art and wit makes a fool of suspicion: pray be wary.

LAXTON

Push, I warrant you:—come, how is't, gallants?

GREENWIT

Pure and excellent.

LAXTON

I thought 'twas good, you were grown so silent; you are like   55
those that love not to talk at victuals, though they make
a worse noise i'the nose than a common fiddler's prentice,

47 *I understand no French* i.e., he declines the innuendo; cf. V.i, 165.

---

41 *the front of a new almanac.* The predictions in almanacs were calculated
for a given meridian, but could be adapted to cover the whole country.

52 *art and wit makes a fool of suspicion.* This sounds proverbial, but appears
not to be otherwise recorded. There is a fairly close parallel in *A Mad
World, My Masters* (I.ii, 93–5): 'The way to daunt is to outvie suspect./
Manage these principles but with art and life,/Welcome all nations,
thou'rt an honest wife'.

and discourse a whole supper with snuffling.—I must speak a
word with you anon.

MISTRESS GALLIPOT

Make your way wisely then.   60

GOSHAWK

Oh what else, sir? he's perfection itself, full of manners, but
not an acre of ground belonging to 'em.

GREENWIT

Ay and full of form, h'as ne'er a good stool in's chamber.

GOSHAWK

But above all religious: he preyeth daily upon elder brothers.

GREENWIT

And valiant above measure: h'as run three streets from a   65
sergeant.

LAXTON

Puh, puh.   *He blows tobacco in their faces*

GREENWIT [*and*] GOSHAWK

Oh, puh, ho, ho.

LAXTON

So, so.

MISTRESS GALLIPOT

What's the matter now, sir?   70

LAXTON

I protest I'm in extreme want of money: if you can supply
me now with any means, you do me the greatest pleasure,
next to the bounty of your love, as ever poor gentleman
tasted.

MISTRESS GALLIPOT

What's the sum would pleasure ye, sir? though you   75
deserve nothing less at my hands.

LAXTON

Why, 'tis but for want of opportunity thou know'st. [*Aside*]
I put her off with opportunity still: by this light I hate her,
but for means to keep me in fashion with gallants: for what I
take from her, I spend upon other wenches, bear her in hand   80

---

61 *manners* with a play on 'manors'
63 *full of form* replete with propriety, with a play on 'form' in the
    sense of bench
76 *nothing less at my hands* i.e., than her love
80 *bear her in hand* deceive her: cf. *Macbeth*, III.i, 80; *Cymbeline*,
    V.v, 43

---

75 *pleasure.* The verb doubtless has here (as currently) the secondary sense
    of stimulate sexually.

still; she has wit enough to rob her husband, and I ways
enough to consume the money.—Why, how now? what? the
chincough?

GOSHAWK

Thou hast the cowardliest trick to come before a man's face
and strangle him ere he be aware: I could find in my heart   85
to make a quarrel in earnest.

LAXTON

Pox, and thou dost—thou know'st I never use to fight with
my friends—thou'll but lose thy labour in't.—Jack Dapper!

Enter J[ACK] DAPPER, *and his man* GULL

GREENWIT

Monsieur Dapper, I dive down to your ankles.

JACK DAPPER

Save ye gentlemen, all three in a peculiar salute.   90

GOSHAWK

He were ill to make a lawyer, he despatches three at once.

LAXTON

So, well said.—But is this of the same tobacco, Mistress
Gallipot?   [*She gives him money secretly*]

MISTRESS GALLIPOT

The same you had at first, sir.

LAXTON

I wish it no better: this will serve to drink at my chamber.   95

GOSHAWK

Shall we taste a pipe on't?

LAXTON

Not of this by my troth, gentlemen, I have sworn before you.

GOSHAWK

What, not Jack Dapper?

LAXTON

Pardon me, sweet Jack, I'm sorry I made such a rash oath,
but foolish oaths must stand: where art going, Jack?   100

JACK DAPPER

Faith, to buy one feather.

LAXTON

[*Aside*] One feather? the fool's peculiar still.

83 *chincough* whooping-cough
94 s.p. MISTRESS GALLIPOT ed. (M. Gal. Q)
95 *drink* smoke (a common expression)

92 *is this of the same tobacco . . .?* 'She gives him money, and he pretends
that he receives only tobacco' (Collier, qu. Bullen).

JACK DAPPER
  Gull.
GULL
  Master?
JACK DAPPER
  Here's three halfpence for your ordinary, boy, meet me an   105
  hour hence in Paul's.
GULL
  [*Aside*] How? three single halfpence? life, this will scarce
  serve a man in sauce, a ha'p'orth of mustard, a ha'p'orth of oil
  and a ha'p'orth of vinegar, what's left then for the pickle
  herring? This shows like small beer i'th' morning after a   110
  great surfeit of wine o'er night: he could spend his three
  pound last night in a supper amongst girls and brave bawdy-
  house boys: I thought his pockets cackled not for nothing,
  these are the eggs of three pound, I'll go sup 'em up
  presently.   *Exit* GULL   115
LAXTON
  [*Aside*] Eight, nine, ten angels: good wench i'faith, and one
  that loves darkness well, she puts out a candle with the best
  tricks of any drugster's wife in England: but that which
  mads her, I rail upon opportunity still, and take no notice
  on't. The other night she would needs lead me into a room   120
  with a candle in her hand to show me a naked picture, where
  no sooner entered but the candle was sent of an errand: now
  I not intending to understand her, but like a puny at the
  inns of venery, called for another light innocently: thus
  reward I all her cunning with simple mistaking. I know she   125
  cozens her husband to keep me, and I'll keep her honest as
  long as I can, to make the poor man some part of amends:
  an honest mind of a whoremaster!—How think you amongst

---

113 *cackled* gave away secrets
122 *errand* ed. (arrant Q)
123 *puny* freshman
128 *whoremaster* womanizer, lecher: cf. *Measure for Measure*, III.ii,
     36

---

105 *three halfpence for your ordinary.* Bullen quotes from *Father Hubburd's
     Tales:* 'we ... took our repast at thrifty Mother Walker's, where we
     found a whole nest of pinching bachelors, crowded together upon
     forms and benches in that most worshipful three halfpenny ordinary'.
106 *Paul's.* i.e., St Paul's, in the nave of which masterless men set up their
     bills for service. (See *Sh. Eng.*, II, 166.)

you? What, a fresh pipe? draw in a thread, man.
GOSHAWK
No, you're a hoarder, you engross by th'ounces.   130
                        At the feather-shop now
JACK DAPPER
Puh, I like it not.
MISTRESS TILTYARD What feather is't you'd have, sir?
These are most worn and most in fashion
Amongst the beaver gallants, the stone riders,
The private stage's audience, the twelvepenny-stool gentle-
                                                          men:
I can inform you 'tis the general feather.   135
JACK DAPPER
And therefore I mislike it—tell me of general!
Now a continual Simon and Jude's rain
Beat all your feathers as flat down as pancakes.
Show me—a—spangled feather.
MISTRESS TILTYARD   Oh, to go
A-feasting with? you'd have it for a hench-boy?   140
You shall.

---

130 *engross* buy up wholesale, especially for reselling at an inflated
    price
130 *by th'* ed. (bith Q)
131 s.p. MISTRESS ed. (M. Q): Master Tiltyard is not present
133 *stone riders* unexplained; but perhaps womanizers
137 *Simon and Jude's rain* cf. I.ii, 201 and note
138 *as flat down as pancakes* proverbial from an early period
140 *hench-boy?* page: punctuation ed. (hinch-boy, Q)

---

129 *draw in a thread, man.* (third man Q) 'Third' is occasionally found for
    'thread', and 'thrid', for which 'third' could be a compositor's slip,
    quite commonly. But this is frankly a guess at a meaning which I cannot
    find in Q as it stands. I suggest that Laxton may be inviting Goshawk to
    draw in (= inhale) a thread of smoke; or 'thread' may be a measure of
    tobacco as of yarn. But 'draw in' can mean inveigle or take in, and also,
    it seems, to lay down a stake at dice (cf. *Michaelmas Term*, II.i, 29).
131–39 These lines are printed as in Q; but perhaps they should be prose.
133 *beaver gallants.* Those wearing beaver hats. Stubbes in the *Anatomy of
    Abuses* refers to beaver hats at 20, 30, and 40 shillings.
134 *The private stage's audience.* 'Private' playhouses were devised to circum-
    vent the regulations of the Act of Common Council which forbade
    houses of public entertainment within the liberties of the City. The
    performances, given by children (who were technically in training),
    were to quite small and select audiences, who paid high prices for
    admission.
134 *twelvepenny-stool.* The normal price for the use of a stool was sixpence.

At the sempster's shop now

MASTER OPENWORK

Mass, I had quite forgot.
His honour's footman was here last night, wife,
Ha' you done with my lord's shirt?

MISTRESS OPENWORK   What's that to you, sir?

I was this morning at his honour's lodging,   145
Ere such a snail as you crept out of your shell.

MASTER OPENWORK

Oh 'twas well done, good wife.

MISTRESS OPENWORK   I hold it better, sir,

Than if you had done't yourself.

MASTER OPENWORK   Nay, so say I:

But is the countess's smock almost done, mouse?

MISTRESS OPENWORK

Here lies the cambric, sir, but wants, I fear me.   150

MASTER OPENWORK

I'll resolve you of that presently.

MISTRESS OPENWORK

Hey-day! oh audacious groom,
Dare you presume to noblewomen's linen?
Keep you your yard to measure shepherd's holland,
I must confine you, I see that.   155

At the tobacco shop now

GOSHAWK

What say you to this gear?

LAXTON

I dare the arrant'st critic in tobacco
To lay one fault upon't.

Enter MOLL *in a frieze jerkin and a black saveguard*

GOSHAWK   Life, yonder's Moll.

LAXTON

Moll, which Moll?

146 *snail* ed. (snake Q)
150 *wants* i.e., wants finishing, or perhaps there isn't enough material
152 *Hey-day!* ed. (Haida Q)
154 *shepherd's holland* linen for shepherds' smocks
156 *gear* stuff; but the (then standard English) sense of genitals may
    be present
157 *arrant'st* ed. (arrants Q) strictest
158 s.d. *saveguard* an outer petticoat worn by women to protect their
    dress when riding

GOSHAWK
    Honest Moll.   160
LAXTON
    Prithee let's call her.—Moll.
ALL [GALLANTS]
    Moll, Moll, pist, Moll.
MOLL
    How now, what's the matter?
GOSHAWK
    A pipe of good tobacco, Moll.
MOLL
    I cannot stay.   165
GOSHAWK
    Nay Moll, puh, prithee hark, but one word i'faith.
MOLL
    Well, what is't?
GREENWIT
    Prithee come hither, sirrah.
LAXTON
    [Aside] Heart, I would give but too much money to be
    nibbling with that wench: life, sh'as the spirit of four great   170
    parishes, and a voice that will drown all the city: methinks a
    brave captain might get all his soldiers upon her, and ne'er be
    beholding to a company of Mile End milksops, if he could
    come on, and come off quick enough: such a Moll were a
    marrow-bone before an Italian, he would cry bona roba till his   175
    ribs were nothing but bone. I'll lay hard siege to her, money

---

172 *get* i.e., beget
175 *bona roba* wench, frequently a prostitute (the term had lately
    been taken over from Italian)

---

173 *Mile End milksops.* The city trained-bands were exercised at Mile
    End; it was also a place of resort for cakes and cream.
175 *marrow-bone before an Italian.* Marrow-bone was popularly supposed to
    be an aphrodisiac. Cf. *A Mad World, My Masters*, I.ii, 46ff: 'I have
    conveyed away all her wanton pamphlets; as *Hero and Leander, Venus
    and Adonis*; O, two luscious marrowbone pies for a young married
    wife!' Italians were widely believed to be extremely lecherous and to be
    fond of unorthodox coital positions. (cf. *Michaelmas Term*, III.i, 18,
    and *A Mad World, My Masters*, III.iii, 59.) Moll's 'masculinity' might
    here imply a suggestion of buggery.

is that aqua fortis that eats into many a maidenhead:
where the walls are flesh and blood, I'll ever pierce through
with a golden auger.

GOSHAWK

Now thy judgment, Moll, is't not good?   180

MOLL

Yes faith 'tis very good tobacco, how do you sell an ounce?
Farewell. God b'i'you, Mistress Gallipot.

GOSHAWK

Why Moll, Moll.

MOLL

I cannot stay now i'faith, I am going to buy a shag ruff, the
shop will be shut in presently.   185

GOSHAWK

'Tis the maddest fantasticall'st girl:—I never knew so much
flesh and so much nimbleness put together.

LAXTON

She slips from one company to another like a fat eel between
a Dutchman's fingers.—[*Aside*] I'll watch my time for her.

MISTRESS GALLIPOT

Some will not stick to say she is a man   190
And some both man and woman.

LAXTON

That were excellent, she might first cuckold the husband and
then make him do as much for the wife.

The feather-shop again

MOLL

Save you; how does Mistress Tiltyard?

JACK DAPPER

Moll.   195

MOLL

Jack Dapper.

JACK DAPPER

How dost Moll?

MOLL

I'll tell thee by and by, I go but to th'next shop.

---

177 *aqua fortis* literally nitric acid, commonly used in dilute form as a
    solvent
177–8 *maidenhead . . . I'll* punctuation ed. (maidenhead, where . . .
    bloud. I'll . . . Q)
184 *shag* cloth having a velvet nap on one side, usually of worsted but
    sometimes of silk
190 *she is* ed. (shees Q)

JACK DAPPER

Thou shalt find me here this hour about a feather.

MOLL

Nay and a feather hold you in play a whole hour, a goose   200
will last you all the days of your life.

The sempster shop

Let me see a good shag ruff.

MASTER OPENWORK

Mistress Mary, that shalt thou i'faith, and the best in the shop.

MISTRESS OPENWORK

How now, greetings, love-terms with a pox between you,
have I found out one of your haunts? I send you for hollands,   205
and you're i'th'low countries with a mischief. I'm served with
good ware by th'shift, that makes it lie dead so long upon
my hands, I were as good shut up shop, for when I open it
I take nothing.

MASTER OPENWORK

Nay and you fall a-ringing once, the devil cannot stop you,   210
I'll out of the belfry as fast as I can.—Moll.

MISTRESS OPENWORK

Get you from my shop.

---

206 *i'th'low* ed. (ith the low Q)
210 *ringing* scolding

205–9 *I send you . . . nothing.* A dazzling linguistic challenge. The first
pun seems to derive in particular from the brilliant wordplay of *2 Henry
IV*, II.ii, 21–2: 'the rest of thy low countries have made a shift to eat up
thy holland': 'low countries' (the first half of the latter word was always
suggestive: see *Hamlet*, III.ii, 120) meant both the lower parts of the
body and the stews (where Poins and supposedly Master Openwork
beget bastards); hence, similarly, 'holland', as well as, literally, linen—
which prompts 'shift' in the sense of chemise. And the seemingly
innocent shopkeeping talk in the second sentence conceals a complex
obscenity: 'ware' was in regular use for the privates of either sex, but
especially of women (where it was commonly 'lady's ware') (cf. *A
Chaste Maid in Cheapside*, II.i, 99). The burden, then, of Mistress
Openwork's complaint is that by a trick (a shift) she is left to make what
shift she can by handling her sexual parts (those next to her shift) herself: a barren ('dead') activity, but she may as well stop offering herself,
for when she opens up her 'shop', nothing comes in.

211 *Moll*. Her name appears at the end of a line seemingly as the last word of
Openwork's speech. But I suspect it may be the speech prefix of a
missing few words from Moll, to which Mistress Openwork's speech is
a retort.

MOLL

I come to buy.

MISTRESS OPENWORK

I'll sell ye nothing, I warn ye my house and shop.

MOLL

You goody Openwork, you that prick out a poor living   215
And sews many a bawdy skin-coat together,
Thou private pandress between shirt and smock,
I wish thee for a minute but a man:
Thou should'st never use more shapes; but as th'art
I pity my revenge: now my spleen's up   220
I would not mock it willingly.

> *Enter a* FELLOW *with a long rapier by his side*
>   —Ha, be thankful,

Now I forgive thee.

MISTRESS OPENWORK   Marry hang thee,

I never asked forgiveness in my life.

MOLL

You, goodman swine's-face.

FELLOW

What, will you murder me?   225

MOLL

You remember, slave, how you abused me t'other night in a
tavern?

FELLOW

Not I, by this light.

MOLL

No, but by candlelight you did, you have tricks to save your
oaths, reservations have you? and I have reserved somewhat   230
for you. [*Strikes him*] As you like that, call for more, you
know the sign again.

FELLOW

Pox on't, had I brought any company along with me to have
borne witness on't, 'twould ne'er have grieved me, but to be
struck and nobody by, 'tis my ill fortune still: why, tread   235

214 *warn* deny
215 *goody* shortened form of 'goodwife', a term of civility used to
    married women of humble station
216 *skin-coat* a coat made of skins, but used figuratively of a person's
    skin itself
221 s.d. FELLOW probably in the sense of thief (cf. *A Trick to Catch
    the Old One*, II.i, 19f.)
235 *tread . . . tail* i.e., even the humblest will resent extreme ill-treat-
    ment: a common proverbial expression

upon a worm, they say 'twill turn tail, but indeed a gentleman
should have more manners.   *Exit* FELLOW

LAXTON

Gallantly performed i'faith Moll, and manfully, I love thee
forever for't: base rogue, had he offered but the least counter-
buff, by this hand I was prepared for him.   240

MOLL

You prepared for him? why should you be prepared for him,
was he any more than a man?

LAXTON

No, nor so much by a yard and a handful London measure.

MOLL

Why do you speak this then? do you think I cannot ride a
stone horse unless one lead him by th'snaffle?   245

LAXTON

Yes and sit him bravely, I know thou canst Moll, 'twas but an
honest mistake through love, and I'll make amends for't
any way: prithee sweet plump Moll, when shall thou and I
go out o'town together?

MOLL

Whither? to Tyburn, prithee?   250

LAXTON

Mass that's out o'town indeed, thou hangst so many jests
upon thy friends still. I mean honestly to Brainford, Staines
or Ware.

MOLL

What to do there?

LAXTON

Nothing but be merry and lie together, I'll hire a coach with   255
four horses.

MOLL

I thought 'twould be a beastly journey: you may leave out

---

243 *London measure* a former practice of London drapers of allowing
    a little more than the standard yard
245 *stone horse* stallion
257 *beastly* obscene; sexually bestial

---

243 For the obscene pun on 'yard' cf. II.ii, 82n.
244 *ride a stone horse.* A stone horse is a stallion, likely to be a horse of some
    spirit; but there is likely to be in Laxton's answer a hint of Moll's
    assumed sexual prowess, though 'to ride a horse' was normally used of a
    man, meaning to mount a woman.
252 *Brainford.* A common spelling of Brentford, then a popular place for
    assignations (as were Staines and Ware), and one of the most fre-
    quently alluded to.

one well, three horses will serve if I play the jade myself.

LAXTON

Nay push, th'art such another kicking wench, prithee be
kind and let's meet. 260

MOLL

'Tis hard but we shall meet, sir.

LAXTON

Nay but appoint the place then, there's ten angels in fair
gold, Moll, you see I do not trifle with you, do but say thou
wilt meet me, and I'll have a coach ready for thee.

MOLL

Why, here's my hand I'll meet you sir. 265

LAXTON

[Aside] Oh good gold.—The place, sweet Moll?

MOLL

It shall be your appointment.

LAXTON

Somewhat near Holborn, Moll.

MOLL

In Gray's Inn Fields then.

LAXTON

A match. 270

MOLL

I'll meet you there.

LAXTON

The hour?

MOLL

Three.

LAXTON

That will be time enough to sup at Brainford.

Fall from them to the other

MASTER OPENWORK

I am of such a nature, sir, I cannot endure the house when 275
she scolds, sh'has a tongue will be heard further in a still

---

258 *play the jade* act the whore: the word was used contemptuously of
  both horses and women
274 s.d. *Fall from them to the other* i.e., the other group on the stage
  come forward or take over the dialogue
276 *heard* ed. (hard Q)

---

269 *Gray's Inn Fields.* Open fields to the north of Gray's Inn, used as an
  archery ground, but afterwards frequented by footpads.

morning than Saint Antling's bell, she rails upon me for
foreign wenching, that I being a freeman must needs keep a
whore i'th'suburbs, and seek to impoverish the liberties:
when we fall out, I trouble you still to make all whole with   280
my wife.

GOSHAWK

No trouble at all, 'tis a pleasure to me to join things together.

MASTER OPENWORK

[*Aside*] Go thy ways, I do this but to try thy honesty,
Goshawk.

The feather shop

JACK DAPPER

How lik'st thou this, Moll?   285

MOLL

Oh singularly, you're fitted now for a bunch. [*Aside*] He
looks for all the world with those spangled feathers like a
nobleman's bedpost. The purity of your wench would I fain
try, she seems, like Kent, unconquered, and I believe as
many wiles are in her—oh, the gallants of these times are   290
shallow lechers, they put not their courtship home enough to
a wench, 'tis impossible to know what woman is thoroughly
honest, because she's ne'er thoroughly tried: I am of that

277 *Saint Antling's bell.* St Antholin's Church, which stood in Watling
Street, near St Paul's, was much frequented by Puritans. In 1599 a
number of clergymen of Puritan views established a morning lecture
here, the bell for which began to ring at 5 a.m. and was a great nuisance
to the neighbourhood (Sugden). The church, rebuilt after the Great
Fire of 1666, was pulled down in 1874.

279 *suburbs.* Those, that is, beyond the liberties of the City. 'Liberties'
meant also rights or privileges, and Master Openwork must be hinting
at those of his wife.

288 *a nobleman's bedpost.* The beds of the wealthy were festooned with rich
hangings.

288 *The purity of your wench would I fain try.* i.e., of Mistress Tiltyard.
'Try' is used frequently by Middleton in a sexual sense. So Deflores
misinterprets Beatrice in *The Changeling* (II.ii, 97ff.). Moll's intention is
not acted upon; since the Tiltyards play so small a part, it may be that
an episode has been cancelled.

289 *like Kent, unconquered.* It was a boast of Kentishmen that Kent had
never been conquered. At Swanscombe (near Northfleet) in 1066, when
William I marched round the county to secure the coast and the Channel
ports, he is traditionally said to have met the men of Kent and confirmed
their possession of all their laws and privileges. The phrase seems
likely to be a direct theft from Drayton, *The Barons' Wars*, I, 323–4:

Then those of Kent, unconquered of the rest,
That to this day maintain their ancient right.

certain belief there are more queans in this town of their
own making than of any man's provoking; where lies the   295
slackness then? many a poor soul would down, and there's
nobody will push 'em:
Women are courted but ne'er soundly tried,
As many walk in spurs that never ride.

The sempster's shop

MISTRESS OPENWORK
Oh abominable.   300

GOSHAWK
Nay more, I tell you in private, he keeps a whore i'th'suburbs.

MISTRESS OPENWORK
Oh spital dealing, I came to him a gentlewoman born. I'll
show you mine arms when you please, sir.

GOSHAWK
[*Aside*] I had rather see your legs, and begin that way.

MISTRESS OPENWORK
'Tis well known he took me from a lady's service, where I   305
was well beloved of the steward, I had my Latin tongue, and
a spice of the French before I came to him, and now doth
he keep a suburbian whore under my nostrils.

GOSHAWK
There's ways enough to cry quit with him: hark in thine ear.

MISTRESS OPENWORK
There's a friend worth a million.   310

MOLL
[*Aside*] I'll try one spear against your chastity, Mistress
Tiltyard, though it prove too short by the burr.

Enter RALPH TRAPDOOR

TRAPDOOR
[*Aside*] Mass, here she is. I'm bound already to serve her,
though it be but a sluttish trick.—Bless my hopeful young

309 *quit* ed. (quite Q: an obsolete form)
312 *burr* (burgh Q) a broad iron ring on a tilting lance, just behind
the place for the hand

---

302 *spital dealing.* Spitals were originally lazar houses, but came to be used
for maimed whores.
306 *my Latin tongue.* These phrases might suggest that Mistress Openwork
had herself been loose before marriage, especially if 'French' is taken
to hint at syphilis. 'Latin tongue' may be another gesture towards
Italian sexual habits.
308 *suburbian* obsolete spelling, commonly used where the reference was to
licentious life there.

mistress with long life and great limbs, send her the upper   315
hand of all bailiffs and their hungry adherents.

MOLL

How now, what art thou?

TRAPDOOR

A poor ebbing gentleman, that would gladly wait for the
young flood of your service.

MOLL

My service! what should move you to offer your service to   320
me, sir?

TRAPDOOR

The love I bear to your heroic spirit and masculine womanhood.

MOLL

So sir, put case we should retain you to us, what parts are
there in you for a gentlewoman's service?   325

TRAPDOOR

Of two kinds, right worshipful: movable and immovable:
movable to run of errands, and immovable to stand when
you have occasion to use me.

MOLL

What strength have you?

TRAPDOOR

Strength, Mistress Moll? I have gone up into a steeple, and   330
stayed the great bell as 't has been ringing; stopped a windmill going.

MOLL

And never struck down yourself?

TRAPDOOR

Stood as upright as I do at this present.

MOLL *trips up his heels, he falls*

MOLL

Come, I pardon you for this, it shall be no disgrace to you: 335

---

334 s.d. here ed. (at l. 332 Q)

---

325 *service*. The word, as Christopher Ricks points out (*E in C*, X (1960),
   296), means copulation as well as the duty of a servant. Together with
   'stand' (cf. I.ii, 56n.) it makes Trapdoor's farmyard intentions plain.
   'Use' also has commonly a sexual meaning of course: so, he will have an
   erection when she needs it.

I have struck up the heels of the high German's size ere now.
What, not stand?

TRAPDOOR

I am of that nature, where I love I'll be at my mistress' foot
to do her service.

MOLL

Why well said, but say your mistress should receive injury, 340
have you the spirit of fighting in you, durst you second her?

TRAPDOOR

Life, I have kept a bridge myself, and drove seven at a time
before me.

MOLL

Ay?

TRAPDOOR

(*Aside*) But they were all Lincolnshire bullocks by my troth. 345

MOLL

Well, meet me in Gray's Inn Fields, between three and four
this afternoon, and upon better consideration we'll retain
you.

TRAPDOOR

I humbly thank your good mistress-ship.
[*Aside*] I'll crack your neck for this kindness. *Exit* TRAPDOOR 350
MOLL *meets* LAXTON

LAXTON

Remember three.

MOLL

Nay if I fail you, hang me.

LAXTON

Good wench i'faith.

then OPENWORK

MOLL

Who's this?

MASTER OPENWORK

'Tis I, Moll. 355

MOLL

Prithee tend thy shop and prevent bastards.

336 *the high German.* There are a number of allusions to the high German,
who was evidently a fencer of great size who seems to have spent some
considerable time in London. In *The Owl's Almanac*, 7, Dekker says
that he 'cudgelled most of our English fencers now about a month past';
in Shirley's *The Opportunity* he has 'beaten all the fencers in Europe';
but he was at one time, it seems, imprisoned, for 'those escape very
hardly, like the German out of Wood-street' (*The Curtain Drawer of
the World* (1612, qu. Collier), 27).

MASTER OPENWORK
> We'll have a pint of the same wine i'faith, Moll.
>> [*Exeunt* MOLL *and* MASTER OPENWORK]
>>> *The bell rings*

GOSHAWK
> Hark the bell rings, come gentlemen.
> Jack Dapper, where shall's all munch?

JACK DAPPER
> I am for Parker's ordinary.   360

LAXTON
> He's a good guest to'm, he deserves his board,
> He draws all the gentlemen in a term-time thither:
> We'll be your followers, Jack, lead the way:
> Look you by my faith the fool has feathered his nest well.
>> *Exeunt* GALLANTS

Enter MASTER GALLIPOT, MASTER TILTYARD, *and* SERVANTS *with water-spaniels and a duck*

MASTER TILTYARD
> Come shut up your shops: where's Master Openwork?   365

MISTRESS GALLIPOT
> Nay ask not me, Master Tiltyard.

MASTER TILTYARD
> Where's his water-dog? puh—pist—hur—hur—pist.

MASTER GALLIPOT
> Come wenches come, we're going all to Hogsden.

MISTRESS GALLIPOT
> To Hogsden, husband?

MASTER GALLIPOT
> Ay, to Hogsden, pigsney.   370

---

357 s.d. *The bell rings* i.e., a clock strikes
360 *Parker's* unidentified
361 *to'm* (stet Q); meaning 'to him' not 'to them'
364 s.d. *duck* i.e., one used as a decoy
367 *puh–pist* . . . cf. l. 372
370 *pigsney* (i.e., pig's eye) darling, pet

---

357 *a pint of the same wine.* Bastard was a sweet Spanish wine resembling Muscadel.
366 s.p. MISTRESS GALLIPOT. Perhaps this speech should be given to Mistress Openwork, to whom the question would be more appropriately put, and from whom the reply would be more pointed.
370 *Hogsden.* i.e., Hoxton, then much resorted to for excursions by citizens and apprentices.

MISTRESS GALLIPOT
 I'm not ready, husband.

MASTER GALLIPOT
 Faith that's well—hum—pist—pist. *Spits in the dog's mouth*
 Come Mistress Openwork, you are so long.

MISTRESS OPENWORK
 I have no joy of my life, Master Gallipot.

MASTER GALLIPOT
 Push, let your boy lead his water-spaniel along, and we'll   375
 show you the bravest sport at Parlous Pond. Hey Trug, hey
 Trug, hey Trug, here's the best duck in England, except my
 wife;
 Hey, hey, hey, fetch, fetch, fetch, come let's away.
 Of all the year this is the sportfull'st day.   [*Exeunt*]   380

[Act II, Scene ii]

Enter SEBASTIAN *solus*

SEBASTIAN
 If a man have a free will, where should the use
 More perfect shine than in his will to love?
 All creatures have their liberty in that,

Enter SIR ALEXANDER *and listens to him*

 Though else kept under servile yoke and fear,
 The very bondslave has his freedom there.   5
 Amongst a world of creatures voiced and silent
 Must my desires wear fetters?—Yea, are you
 So near? then I must break with my heart's truth,

5 *there.* ed. (there, Q)
6 *silent.* ed. (silent. Q)
7 *fetters?* ed. (fetters— Q)

---

372 s.d. *Spits in the dog's mouth.* The reason for this action is obscure.
  Mr T. R. Henn suggests that it may have been a device to ensure that
  the dog memorized its master's scent; he also informs me that he has
  known gamekeepers to spit on a ferret after it has been muzzled to
  smooth down the fur ruffled by the muzzle. Possibly the dog was
  similarly muzzled.
376 *Parlous Pond.* Parlous or Perilous Pool (so called because it was the
  scene of many accidents) was a large pond lying behind St Luke's
  Hospital on the edge of Hoxton; it was a favourite place for duck-
  hunting and later for bathing. Though both 'pond' and 'sport' make
  sexual openings, it seems to be literal wildfowl that the citizens are
  going after.

Meet grief at a back way.—Well: why, suppose
The two-leaved tongues of slander or of truth   10
Pronounce Moll loathsome: if before my love
She appear fair, what injury have I?
I have the thing I like: in all things else
Mine own eye guides me, and I find 'em prosper:
Life, what should ail it now? I know that man   15
Ne'er truly loves—if he gainsay't he lies—
That winks and marries with his father's eyes.
I'll keep mine own wide open.

Enter MOLL *and a* PORTER *with a viol on his back*

SIR ALEXANDER   Here's brave wilfulness,
A made match, here she comes, they met o'purpose.
PORTER
Must I carry this great fiddle to your chamber, Mistress   20
Mary?
MOLL
Fiddle, goodman hog-rubber? Some of these porters bear so
much for others, they have no time to carry wit for
themselves.
PORTER
To your own chamber, Mistress Mary?   25

---

9 *why, suppose* ed. (why suppose. Q)
22 *hog-rubber* used as a term of contempt, probably not clearly
distinguished from 'hog-grubber', a mean or sneaking fellow

---

10 *two-leaved* ed. (two leaud Q) After some hesitation I follow Dyce and
later editors. Collier suggested 'lewd', for which 'leaud' is a recorded
contemporary spelling (Holland's *Pliny*, 1601, I, 31), and we should
presumably then understand it in the sense of unlearned or ignorant.
Bowers explains 'two-leaved' as a 'comparison of the tongue to the two
hinged parts of a door or gate, [i.e. equivalent to the Latin *valvae*; cf
Isaiah XLV, 1] each of which can move independently and thus pronounce either slander or truth', and he gives 'double-tongued' as a
modern equivalent. The aptness of the comparison is uncompelling,
though the singular 'tongue' would improve matters. But this reading
may be preferred.

22 *Fiddle.* There is evidently some joke here which I haven't been able to
uncover. By the 18th century, 'fiddle' had become one of many words
for the female sexual organs, and it could also mean a writ to arrest;
but neither seems to have much appropriateness here. cf., however,
Henry VIII, I.iii, 38–40: 'The sly whoresons/Have got a speeding
trick to lay down ladies;/A French song and a fiddle has no fellow'.

MOLL

Who'll hear an ass speak? Whither else, goodman pageant-
bearer? they're people of the worst memories. *Exit* PORTER

SEBASTIAN

Why, 'twere too great a burthen, love, to have them carry
things in their minds and o'their backs together.

MOLL

Pardon me sir, I thought not you so near. 30

SIR ALEXANDER

So, so, so.

SEBASTIAN

I would be nearer to thee, and in that fashion
That makes the best part of all creatures honest.
No otherwise I wish it.

MOLL

Sir, I am so poor to requite you, you must look for nothing 35
but thanks of me: I have no humour to marry, I love to lie
o' both sides o'th'bed myself, and again o'th'other side; a
wife you know ought to be obedient, but I fear me I am too
headstrong to obey, therefore I'll ne'er go about it. I love you
so well, sir, for your good will I'd be loath you should repent 40
your bargain after, and therefore we'll ne'er come together at
first. I have the head now of myself, and am man enough for a
woman; marriage is but a chopping and changing, where a
maiden loses one head and has a worse i'th'place.

SIR ALEXANDER

The most comfortablest answer from a roaring girl 45
That ever mine ears drunk in.

SEBASTIAN   This were enough

Now to affright a fool forever from thee,
When 'tis the music that I love thee for.

SIR ALEXANDER

There's a boy spoils all again.

MOLL

Believe it, sir, I am not of that disdainful temper, but I could 50
love you faithfully.

SIR ALEXANDER

A pox on you for that word. I like you not now,

---

41 *at first* in the first place

26 *pageant-bearer.* A pageant was a portable stage, consisting of boards
resting on a framework of trestles, which could be set up in the street
for the acting of plays or other spectacles. I do not know why pageant-
bearers should have been noted for forgetfulness.

Y'are a cunning roarer. I see that already.

MOLL

But sleep upon this once more, sir, you may chance shift a
mind tomorrow: be not too hasty to wrong yourself, never   55
while you live, sir, take a wife running, many have run out at
heels that have done't: you see, sir, I speak against myself,
and if every woman would deal with their suitor so honestly,
poor younger brothers would not be so often gulled with old
cozening widows, that turn o'er all their wealth in trust to   60
some kinsman, and make the poor gentleman work hard for
a pension. Fare you well sir.

SEBASTIAN

Nay prithee one word more.

SIR ALEXANDER

How do I wrong this girl, she puts him off still.

MOLL

Think upon this in cold blood, sir, you make as much haste   65
as if you were going upon a sturgeon voyage, take delibera-
tion, sir, never choose a wife as if you were going to Virginia.

SEBASTIAN

And so we parted, my too cursed fate.

SIR ALEXANDER

She is but cunning, gives him longer time in't.

Enter a TAILOR

TAILOR

Mistress Moll, Mistress Moll: so ho ho so ho.   70

66 *a sturgeon voyage.* OED can only suggest a voyage for sturgeon, which
 scarcely explains what Moll means; probably, like the reference to
 Virginia, the allusion is to a voyage of long duration for which a wife
 would be much-desired company. But sturgeons were found in the
 Thames, and the Lord Mayor had the right to all caught above London
 Bridge.
67 *as if you were going to Virginia.* Presumably because there would be no
 chance of finding a wife once there, one must take one from home; but
 there may be an obscure play on the name of the colony. And cf.
 Thomas Harvey's exploits mentioned above, p. ix.
68 Dyce suggests a quotation here, but none has been located.
70 *so ho ho so ho.* This is a customary falconer's cry, encouraging the bird
 to stoop to the lure. Hence 'hawking' in the next line, and perhaps the
 'red clout'. The lure was a bunch of feathers sewn on to cloth, sometimes with a piece of red meat in the middle; in the tailor's case the
 'clout' seems likely to have been a pincushion worn strapped to the
 wrist or finger. 'There boy' was a huntsman's cry to his dogs: cf. *The
 Tempest*, IV.i, 256.

MOLL

There boy, there boy, what, dost thou go a-hawking after
me with a red clout on thy finger?

TAILOR

I forgot to take measure on you for your new breeches.

SIR ALEXANDER

Hoyda, breeches? what, will he marry a monster with two
trinkets? What age is this? if the wife go in breeches, the man   75
must wear long coats like a fool.

MOLL

What fiddling's here? would not the old pattern have served
your turn?

TAILOR

You change the fashion, you say you'll have the great Dutch
slop, Mistress Mary.   80

MOLL

Why sir, I say so still.

TAILOR

Your breeches then will take up a yard more.

MOLL

Well, pray look it be put in then.

TAILOR

It shall stand round and full, I warrant you.

MOLL

Pray make 'em easy enough.   85

TAILOR

I know my fault now, t'other was somewhat stiff between the
legs, I'll make these open enough, I warrant you.

SIR ALEXANDER

Here's good gear towards, I have brought up my son to
marry a Dutch slop and a French doublet, a codpiece-
daughter.   90

---

76 *coats* sc. petticoats
77 *fiddling* fidgeting, playing about
79 *great Dutch slop* wide baggy breeches, then newly in fashion
88 *gear* clothing, with a secondary sense of business at hand

---

74–5 *two trinkets*. No slang or cant use is recorded. 'Trinkets' may mean
testicles or (taking account of 'monster') suggest that he thinks her
bisexual with the organs of both.

82 This and the tailor's next three speeches have an obscene pun on 'yard'
(= penis, as at *Love's Labour's Lost*, V.ii, 663). cf. *The Honest Whore*,
part 1, V.ii, 259ff.: 'This was her tailor—you cut out her loose-bodied
gown, and put in a yard more than I allowed her'.

TAILOR

So, I have gone as far as I can go.

MOLL

Why then, farewell.

TAILOR

If you go presently to your chamber, Mistress Mary, pray
send me the measure of your thigh by some honest body.

MOLL

Well sir, I'll send it by a porter presently.   *Exit* MOLL   95

TAILOR

So you had need, it is a lusty one, both of them would make
any porter's back ache in England.   *Exit* TAILOR

SEBASTIAN

I have examined the best part of man,
Reason and judgment, and in love they tell me
They leave me uncontrolled: he that is swayed   100
By an unfeeling blood past heat of love,
His springtime must needs err, his watch ne'er goes right
That sets his dial by a rusty clock.

SIR ALEXANDER

So, and which is that rusty clock, sir, you?

SEBASTIAN

The clock at Ludgate, sir, it ne'er goes true.   105

SIR ALEXANDER

But thou goest falser: not thy father's cares
Can keep thee right. When that insensible work
Obeys the workman's art, lets off the hour
And stops again when time is satisfied:
But thou run'st on, and judgment, thy main wheel,   110

96 *a lusty one.* Thighs are an obvious incitement to sexual adventure. cf.
     Romeo and Juliet II.i, 19f.: Rosaline's 'quivering thigh,/And the
     demesnes that there adjacent lie'.

100–3 *he that is swayed . . . rusty clock.* This seems to be a rather laboured
     attempt to combine a sardonic comment on the old man's incapacity—
     once he is old and impotent he cannot hope for sexual success, his spring
     is no longer taut, his action is rusty, his rhythm erratic and weak—
     with a warning that the young (those in their springtime) be not ruled
     by the dicta of the elderly.

105 *The clock at Ludgate.* Perhaps the clock on St Martin's Church. Old
     engravings show no clock on the gate itself, which (a replacement of the
     original) was rebuilt in 1586.

107–9 *When that insensible work . . . satisfied.* When the invisible movement
     (of the clock) obeys the workman's art, the hour strikes and stops again
     after the correct number of strokes. (Lets off = removes the stop from
     the strike.)

Beats by all stops, as if the work would break,
Begun with long pains for a minute's ruin:
Much like a suffering man brought up with care,
At last bequeathed to shame and a short prayer.

SEBASTIAN

I taste you bitterer than I can deserve, sir.   115

SIR ALEXANDER

Who has bewitched thee, son? What devil or drug
Hath wrought upon the weakness of thy blood,
And betrayed all her hopes to ruinous folly?
Oh wake from drowsy and enchanted shame,
Wherein thy soul sits with a golden dream   120
Flattered and poisoned. I am old, my son,
Oh let me prevail quickly,
For I have weightier business of mine own
Than to chide thee: I must not to my grave
As a drunkard to his bed, whereon he lies   125
Only to sleep, and never cares to rise.
Let me despatch in time, come no more near her.

SEBASTIAN

Not honestly? not in the way of marriage?

SIR ALEXANDER

What sayst thou, marriage? in what place? the sessions
house? and who shall give the bride, prithee? an indictment?   130

SEBASTIAN

Sir, now ye take part with the world to wrong her.

SIR ALEXANDER

Why, wouldst thou fain marry to be pointed at?
Alas the number's great, do not o'erburden't:
Why, as good marry a beacon on a hill,
Which all the country fix their eyes upon,   135
As her thy folly doats on. If thou long'st
To have the story of thy infamous fortunes
Serve for discourse in ordinaries and taverns,
Th'art in the way: or to confound thy name,
Keep on, thou canst not miss it: or to strike   140
Thy wretched father to untimely coldness,

---

114 *short prayer* sc. before execution: cf. III.i, 117
116 *bewitched* ed. (bewitch Q)

---

111 *Beats by all stops.* See the previous note; but a stop is also a device to
   prevent overwinding.
118 *all her hopes.* Blood may be thought of as feminine by analogy with
   soul; or possibly we should read 'my' or 'thy'.

Keep the left hand still, it will bring thee to't.
Yet if no tears wrung from thy father's eyes,
Nor sighs that fly in sparkles from his sorrows,
Had power to alter what is wilful in thee,   145
Methinks her very name should fright thee from her,
And never trouble me.
SEBASTIAN
Why is the name of Moll so fatal, sir?
SIR ALEXANDER
Marry, one, sir, where suspect is entered,
For seek all London from one end to t'other,   150
More whores of that name than of any ten other.
SEBASTIAN
What's that to her? let those blush for themselves.
Can any guilt in others condemn her?
I've vowed to love her: let all storms oppose me,
That ever beat against the breast of man,   155
Nothing but death's black tempest shall divide us.
SIR ALEXANDER
Oh folly that can doat on nought but shame!
SEBASTIAN
Put case a wanton itch runs through one name
More than another, is that name the worse,
Where honesty sits possessed in't? it should rather   160
Appear more excellent, and deserve more praise,
When through foul mists a brightness it can raise.
Why, there are of the devil's, honest gentlemen,
And well descended, keep an open house,
And some o'th'good man's that are arrant knaves.   165
He hates unworthily that by rote contemns,
For the name neither saves, nor yet condemns:
And for her honesty, I have made such proof on't,
In several forms, so nearly watched her ways,

158 *Put case* suppose, perhaps with a pun on 'case' meaning vagina
     (as in *A Chaste Maid in Cheapside*, II.i, 199)
163 *of the devil's* among those who appear to be of the devil's party

---

142 *Keep the left hand still.* Act perversely, or perhaps in feigned friendship
     only: the date seems too early for an allusion to left-handed or mor-
     ganatic marriage.
149 *Marry, one, sir, where suspect is entered* ed. (Many one . . . Q) Entered,
     that is, as a presumption in law, one which is presumptively suspicious.
     Possibly we should read 'Marry, 'tis one . . .'
165 *o'th'good man's.* An allusion to the proverb 'God is a good man'. cf.
     Much Ado, III.v, 36.

I will maintain that strict against an army,   170
Excepting you my father: here's her worst,
Sh'has a bold spirit that mingles with mankind,
But nothing else comes near it: and oftentimes
Through her apparel somewhat shames her birth,
But she is loose in nothing but in mirth: 175
Would all Molls were no worse.

SIR ALEXANDER
This way I toil in vain and give but aim
To infamy and ruin: he will fall,
My blessing cannot stay him: all my joys
Stand at the brink of a devouring flood   180
And will be wilfully swallowed: wilfully.
But why so vain let all these tears be lost?
I'll pursue her to shame, and so all's crossed.
                                        Exit SIR ALEXANDER

SEBASTIAN
He is gone with some strange purpose, whose effect
Will hurt me little if he shoot so wide,   185
To think I love so blindly: I but feed
His heart to this match, to draw on th'other,
Wherein my joy sits with a full wish crowned,
Only his mood excepted, which must change
By opposite policies, courses indirect: 190
Plain dealing in this world takes no effect.
This mad girl I'll acquaint with my intent,
Get her assistance, make my fortunes known:
'Twixt lovers' hearts she's a fit instrument,
And has the art to help them to their own: 195
By her advice, for in that craft she's wise,
My love and I may meet, spite of all spies.
                                        Exit SEBASTIAN

189 *change* ed. (change. Q)

177 *give but aim.* The man who gave aim stood near the butt and showed how
   far the arrow fell from the mark.

[Act III, Scene i]

Enter LAXTON *in Gray's Inn Fields with the* COACHMAN

LAXTON
Coachman.

COACHMAN
Here sir.

LAXTON
There's a tester more, prithee drive thy coach to the hither
end of Marybone Park, a fit place for Moll to get in.

COACHMAN
Marybone Park, sir.   5

LAXTON
Ay, it's in our way thou know'st.

COACHMAN
It shall be done, sir.

LAXTON
Coachman.

COACHMAN
Anon, sir.

LAXTON
Are we fitted with good frampold jades?   10

COACHMAN
The best in Smithfield, I warrant you, sir.

---

3 *tester* sixpence (from the teston of Henry VIII, originally worth
 a shilling, and so called because it carried an image of the king's
 head)
10 *frampold* (phrampell Q) mettlesome, spirited
10 *jades* contemptuous term for horses
11 *you* ed. (your Q)

---

4 *Marybone Park*. Until 1611 Marylebone Manor was crown property:
  the gardens (ultimately incorporated into Regent's Park) were said in
  A Fair Quarrel (IV.iv, 217ff.) to be suitable as a burial ground for
  whores and panders because it was near Tyburn. The point of Laxton's
  quip, however, is enriched by the linking of a pun on Marybone (=
  marrow-bone; cf. II.i, 175n.) and park in the sense of 'the female body
  as a domain where the lover may freely roam' (*Sh. Bawdy*, 163; cf.
  Venus and Adonis, 231ff.).
11 *Smithfield*. The worst jades came from Smithfield. cf. *2 Henry IV*,
  I.ii, 50ff., and the proverbial 'Who goes to Westminster for a wife, to
  Paul's for a man, and to Smithfield for a horse, may meet with a whore,
  a knave, and a jade'.

LAXTON

    May we safely take the upper hand of any couched velvet cap
or tufftaffety jacket? for they keep a vild swaggering in
coaches nowadays, the highways are stopped with them.

COACHMAN

    My life for yours, and baffle 'em too sir:—why, they are the   15
same jades, believe it, sir, that have drawn all your famous
whores to Ware.

LAXTON

    Nay, then they know their business, they need no more
instructions.

COACHMAN

    They're so used to such journeys, sir, I never use whip to   20
'em; for if they catch but the scent of a wench once, they
run like devils.

                             Exit COACHMAN *with his whip*

LAXTON

    Fine Cerberus, that rogue will have the start of a thousand
ones, for whilst others trot afoot, he'll ride prancing to hell
upon a coach-horse.   25
    Stay, 'tis now about the hour of her appointment, but yet
I see her not. (*The clock strikes three*) Hark what's this? one,
two, three, three by the clock at Savoy: this is the hour, and
Gray's Inn Fields the place, she swore she'd meet me: ha,
yonder's two Inns o' Court men with one wench, but that's   30
not she, they walk toward Islington out of my way: I see none
yet dressed like her, I must look for a shag ruff, a frieze jerkin,
a short sword, and a saveguard, or I get none: why, Moll,
prithee make haste, or the coachman will curse us anon.

Enter MOLL *like a man*

12 *couched* ed. (coacht Q) embroidered with gold
13 *tufftaffety* a kind of taffeta with pile or nap arranged in tufts
13 *vild* vile
15 *baffle* pass contemptuously
23 *Cerberus* watchdog
33 *saveguard* see II.i, 158n.

12–14 These are the bourgeois nouveaux riches, expensively dressed and
    blocking up the highways by showy but incompetent driving.
28 *Savoy.* The great palace, built originally by Simon de Montfort in 1245
    and reconstructed as a hospital in 1509, was by 1580 the subject of
    complaints that it was used as a nursery by 'great numbers of idle wicked
    persons, cutpurses, cozeners and such other thieves': see G. L. Gomme,
    London (1914), 225.

MOLL

    [*Aside*] Oh here's my gentleman: if they would keep their   35
days as well with their mercers as their hours with their harlots, no bankrupt would give seven score pound for a
sergeant's place, for would you know a catchpoll rightly
derived, the corruption of a citizen is the generation of a sergeant. How his eye hawks for venery!—Come, are you ready,   40
sir?

LAXTON

    Ready? for what, sir?

MOLL

    Do you ask that now, sir? why was this meeting 'pointed?

LAXTON

    I thought you mistook me, sir, you seem to be
    Some young barrister: 45
    I have no suit in law—all my land's sold,
    I praise heaven for't; 't has rid me of much trouble.

MOLL

    Then I must wake you, sir, where stands the coach?

LAXTON

    Who's this? Moll, honest Moll?

MOLL

    So young, and purblind? you're an old wanton in your eyes,   50
    I see that.

LAXTON

    Th'art admirably suited for the Three Pigeons at Brainford,
    I'll swear I know thee not.

MOLL

    I'll swear you did not: but you shall know me now.

LAXTON

    No, not here, we shall be spied i'faith, the coach is better,   55
    come.

MOLL

    Stay.

---

38 *catchpoll* sheriff's officer, especially a bum-bailiff
39 *corruption* decomposition, ceasing to exist

35–8 The construction is somewhat obscure, though the general meaning is
    clear: if men were as prompt in paying their mercers' bills as in keeping
    assignments with harlots, it would be worth no one's while to buy a
    sergeant's place at an inflated price, for there would no longer be the
    bankruptcies to provide him a living.
52 *Three Pigeons*. A well-known inn at Brentford, at one time kept by the
    famous actor John Lowin. It is mentioned in *The Alchemist*, V.iv, 89
    and in other plays.

LAXTON

What, wilt thou untruss a point, Moll?

She puts off her cloak and draws

MOLL

Yes, here's the point that I untruss, 't has but one tag, 'twill
serve, though, to tie up a rogue's tongue.   60

LAXTON

How?

MOLL

There's the gold
With which you hired your hackney, here's her pace,
She racks hard, and perhaps your bones will feel it:
Ten angels of mine own I've put to thine,   65
Win 'em and wear 'em.

LAXTON   Hold Moll, Mistress Mary.

MOLL

Draw, or I'll serve an execution on thee
Shall lay thee up till doomsday.

LAXTON

Draw upon a woman? why, what dost mean, Moll?

MOLL

To teach thy base thoughts manners: th'art one of those   70
That thinks each woman thy fond flexible whore:
If she but cast a liberal eye upon thee,
Turn back her head, she's thine: or, amongst company,
By chance drink first to thee, then she's quite gone,

---

58 *untruss a point* unfasten a tag of doublet or breeches (as for sexual
intercourse: see *Measure for Measure*, III.ii, 181f.)

58 s.d. *draws* sc. her sword

63 *hackney* horse kept for hire, figuratively a prostitute: cf. *The
Honest Whore*, part 1, II.i, 225f.

63 *pace* her training as a whore (cf. *Pericles*, IV.v, 62)

64 *racks* moves with the gait called a rack 'in which the two feet on
each side are lifted almost simultaneously, and the body is left
entirely without support between the lifting of one pair and the
landing of the other' (*OED*)

---

66 *Win 'em and wear 'em.* A popular proverbial expression, often taking the
form 'Win her and wear her' (sc. as a bride).

67 *Draw, or I'll serve an execution on thee.* To serve an execution is to make
formal delivery of a process at law. But in addition to her obvious
threat of punishing him capitally, Moll's words punningly mock the
frustration of Laxton's lecherous intentions; for to draw meant also to
expose the penis (as a sword from a scabbard), and an execution a
performance of the sexual act (see *Troilus and Cressida*, III.ii, 81, and
cf. below, l. 118). Her threat therefore is that she will geld him.

There's no means to help her: nay for a need,   75
Wilt swear unto thy credulous fellow lechers
That thou art more in favour with a lady
At first sight than her monkey all her lifetime.
How many of our sex, by such as thou
Have their good thoughts paid with a blasted name   80
That never deserved loosely or did trip
In path of whoredom beyond cup and lip?
But for the stain of conscience and of soul,
Better had women fall into the hands
Of an act silent than a bragging nothing,   85
There's no mercy in't.—What durst move you, sir,
To think me whorish?—a name which I'd tear out
From the high German's throat if it lay ledger there
To despatch privy slanders against me.
In thee I defy all men, their worst hates,   90
And their best flatteries, all their golden witchcrafts,
With which they entangle the poor spirits of fools.
Distressed needlewomen and trade-fallen wives,
Fish that must needs bite or themselves be bitten,
Such hungry things as these may soon be took   95
With a worm fastened on a golden hook:

77 *thou art* ed. (th'art Q)
77–8 lineation ed. (That th'art . . . first sight/Then her . . . Q)
82 *beyond cup and lip* beyond sharing a loving-cup and kissing
88 *high German's throat* cf. II.i, 336n.
88 *lay ledger* rested permanent, as a fixture
92 *entangle the poor spirits of fools* i.e., endanger their souls by tempting them to sin
92 *fools*. ed. (fooles, Q)   93 *wives*, ed. (wiues. Q)

78 *her monkey*. Monkeys were popular as pets (and proverbially lascivious); but perhaps the word is here used to mean favourite, though this sense seems not to be otherwise recorded. cf., however, the apparently rather nasty quip in *Michaelmas Term*, I.i, 299, 'As an old lady delights in a page or monkey'.
84–5 cf. Shakespeare, Sonnet CXXI:
       'Tis better to be vile than vile esteemed,
       When not to be receives reproach of being;
       And the just pleasure lost, which is so deemed
       Not by our feeling, but by others' seeing.
'Act' here (as, e.g., at *Merchant of Venice*, I.iii, 81) = the act of procreation.
96 To angle with a golden hook is an ancient proverbial expression: cf. *A Fair Quarrel*, III.ii, 123: 'Thou'st fished with silver hooks and golden baits'. 'Fish' was common contemptuous slang for women.

Those are the lecher's food, his prey, he watches
For quarrelling wedlocks, and poor shifting sisters,
'Tis the best fish he takes: but why, good fisherman,
Am I thought meat for you, that never yet   100
Had angling rod cast towards me? 'cause, you'll say,
I'm given to sport, I'm often merry, jest:
Had mirth no kindred in the world but lust?
Oh shame take all her friends then: but howe'er
Thou and the baser world censure my life,   105
I'll send 'em word by thee, and write so much
Upon thy breast, 'cause thou shalt bear't in mind:
Tell them 'twere base to yield, where I have conquered.
I scorn to prostitute myself to a man,
I that can prostitute a man to me,   110
And so I greet thee.

LAXTON   Hear me.

MOLL   Would the spirits
Of all my slanderers were clasped in thine,
That I might vex an army at one time.

LAXTON

I do repent me, hold.   *They fight*

MOLL

You'll die the better Christian then.   115

LAXTON

I do confess I have wronged thee, Moll.

MOLL

Confession is but poor amends for wrong,
Unless a rope would follow.

LAXTON   I ask thee pardon.

98 *wedlocks* i.e., wives
107 *'cause* so that
108 *them* sc. lechers' future victims
112 *slanderers* ed. (slanders Q)

98 *poor shifting sisters*. Perhaps frustrated spinsters, those (not necessarily
literal sisters) who are neglected and make what shift they can; but
'shifting' may suggest those who 'shift beds', i.e., are promiscuous: cf.
A Trick to Catch the Old One, V.ii, 167.
103 *Had*. Perhaps we should read 'Hath' (unless the clause is subordinate
to what follows): 'Had' may have been attracted by the same word two
lines above. The line might, however, be a hypothetical, subordinate to
the following clause.
117 *Confession*. Moll picks up the word in the sense of auricular confession
(cf. I.i, 36n.), which would precede the shriving of a condemned man
immediately before execution. cf. II.ii, 114.

MOLL

I'm your hired whore, sir.

LAXTON

I yield both purse and body.

MOLL   Both are mine,   120

And now at my disposing.

LAXTON   Spare my life.

MOLL

I scorn to strike thee basely.

LAXTON

Spoke like a noble girl, i'faith.

    Heart, I think I fight with a familiar, or the ghost of a
fencer, sh'has wounded me gallantly: call you this a lecher-   125
ous voyage? Here's blood would have served me this seven
year in broken heads and cut fingers, and it now runs all out
together. Pox o' the Three Pigeons, I would the coach were
here now to carry me to the chirurgeons.   *Exit* LAXTON

MOLL

If I could meet my enemies one by one thus,   130
I might make pretty shift with 'em in time,
And make 'em know, she that has wit and spirit
May scorn
To live beholding to her body for meat,
Or for apparel, like your common dame   135
That makes shame get her clothes to cover shame.
Base is that mind that kneels unto her body,
As if a husband stood in awe on's wife;
My spirit shall be mistress of this house,
As long as I have time in't.—Oh,   140

Enter TRAPDOOR

Here comes my man that would be: 'tis his hour.
Faith, a good well-set fellow, if his spirit
Be answerable to his umbles; he walks stiff,
But whether he will stand to't stiffly, there's the point;
Has a good calf for't, and ye shall have many a woman   145
Choose him she means to make her head by his calf;

126 *voyage* ed. (viage Q: an obsolete form)
133–4 lineation ed. (one line Q)
135 *common* sc. to the whole town
143 *answerable to his umbles* in accord with his insides, or rather, here,
     the figure he makes (umbles are the edible inward parts of an
     animal, especially deer)
146 *make* ed. (meke Q)

I do not know their tricks in't. Faith, he seems
A man without; I'll try what he is within.

TRAPDOOR
She told me Gray's Inn Fields 'twixt three and four,
I'll fit her mistress-ship with a piece of service,   150
I'm hired to rid the town of one mad girl.   *She jostles him*
What a pox ails you, sir?

MOLL
He begins like a gentleman.

TRAPDOOR
Heart, is the field so narrow, or your eyesight?
Life, he comes back again.   *She comes towards him* 155

MOLL
Was this spoke to me, sir?

TRAPDOOR
I cannot tell, sir.

MOLL
Go, y'are a coxcomb.

TRAPDOOR
Coxcomb?

MOLL
Y'are a slave.   160

TRAPDOOR
I hope there's law for you, sir.

MOLL
Yea, do you see, sir?   *Turn his hat*

TRAPDOOR
Heart, this is no good dealing, pray let me know what house
you're of.

MOLL
One of the Temple, sir.   *Fillips him* 165

TRAPDOOR
Mass, so methinks.

MOLL
And yet sometime I lie about Chick Lane.

TRAPDOOR
I like you the worse because you shift your lodging so often:
I'll not meddle with you for that trick, sir.

147 *their tricks in't* how they do it   162 *Yea* ed. (Ye Q)
165 s.d. *Fillips him* flicks him with her finger

---

167 *Chick Lane.* Later called West Street: a particularly infamous lurking-
place of thieves in the notorious area around Turnmill Street between
Clerkenwell Green and Smithfield.

MOLL

A good shift, but it shall not serve your turn.   170

TRAPDOOR

You'll give me leave to pass about my business, sir.

MOLL

Your business? I'll make you wait on me before I ha' done,
and glad to serve me too.

TRAPDOOR

How sir? serve you? not if there were no more men in
England.   175

MOLL

But if there were no more women in England, I hope you'd
wait upon your mistress then.

TRAPDOOR

Mistress!

MOLL

Oh you're a tried spirit at a push, sir.

TRAPDOOR

What would your worship have me do?   180

MOLL

You a fighter?

TRAPDOOR

No, I praise heaven, I had better grace and more manners.

MOLL

As how, I pray, sir?

TRAPDOOR

Life, 't had been a beastly part of me to have drawn my
weapons upon my mistress, all the world would 'a' cried   185
shame of me for that.

MOLL

Why, but you knew me not.

TRAPDOOR

Do not say so, mistress. I knew you by your wide straddle,
as well as if I had been in your belly.

MOLL

Well, we shall try you further, i'th'meantime we give you   190
entertainment.

TRAPDOOR

Thank your good mistress-ship.

---

190 *give you entertainment* take you into our service

---

188 *your wide straddle.* Apparently simply a characteristic of Moll's (a habit
of standing with her feet wide astride), for as an attempt at a sexual sally
it seems too clumsy even for Trapdoor.

MOLL

How many suits have you?

TRAPDOOR

No more suits than backs, mistress.

MOLL

Well, if you deserve, I cast off this next week, 195
And you may creep into't.

TRAPDOOR Thank your good worship.

MOLL

Come follow me to St Thomas Apostle's,
I'll put a livery cloak upon your back
The first thing I do.

TRAPDOOR I follow my dear mistress.

Exeunt omnes

[Act III, Scene ii]

Enter MISTRESS GALLIPOT *as from supper, her husband after her*

MASTER GALLIPOT

What Pru, nay sweet Prudence.

MISTRESS GALLIPOT

What a pruing keep you, I think the baby would have a teat
it kyes so: pray be not so fond of me, leave your city humours,
I'm vexed at you to see how like a calf you come bleating after
me. 5

MASTER GALLIPOT

Nay, honey Pru: how does your rising up before all the table
show? and flinging from my friends so uncivilly? Fie Pru, fie,
come.

---

195 *this* i.e., this suit that she is wearing

---

194 *backs.* Bullen prints 'blacks'—presumably a misprint.
197 *St Thomas Apostle's.* The church was east of St Paul's, near College
Hill: it was not rebuilt after the fire. The street in which it stood was the
resort of fishermen and famous for fish dinners; clothiers' shops were in
the neighbourhood.
  2 *pruing.* There is conceivably a play on the dialect word 'proo', which
means to call an animal to a stand.
  3 *kyes.* i.e., cries. Steevens suggests that this is baby-talk (the word is not
in *OED*): 'she imitates the jargon talked by nurses to infants'. Presumably Master Gallipot is the baby.

MISTRESS GALLIPOT
Then up and ride, i'faith.

MASTER GALLIPOT
Up and ride? Nay, my pretty Pru, that's far from my thought,   10
duck: why, mouse, thy mind is nibbling at something, what
is't? what lies upon thy stomach?

MISTRESS GALLIPOT
Such an ass as you: hoyda, y'are best turn midwife, or
physician: y'are a pothecary already, but I'm none of your
drugs.   15

MASTER GALLIPOT
Thou art a sweet drug, sweetest Pru, and the more thou art
pounded, the more precious.

MISTRESS GALLIPOT
Must you be prying into a woman's secrets: say ye?

MASTER GALLIPOT
Woman's secrets?

MISTRESS GALLIPOT
What? I cannot have a qualm come upon me but your teeth   20
waters till your nose hang over it.

MASTER GALLIPOT
It is my love, dear wife.

MISTRESS GALLIPOT
Your love? your love is all words; give me deeds, I cannot
abide a man that's too fond over me, so cookish; thou dost
not know how to handle a woman in her kind.   25

MASTER GALLIPOT
No, Pru? why, I hope I have handled—

MISTRESS GALLIPOT
Handle a fool's head of your own,—fie—fie.

11 *what is't* ed. (whats ist Q)
20 *teeth waters* a variant form of 'mouth waters'
24 *cookish* like a cook, perhaps a nonce word
25 *in her kind* as she deserves, as is proper
27 *fool's head* head empty of sense, perhaps again with a sexual
double entendre

---

9 *ride*. Is Mistress Gallipot picking up a sexual suggestion in her husband's last word and possibly in 'honey' as well? Certainly it seems
there in her next speech. 'Ride' was Standard English for sexual intercourse (cf. below, l.180).
15 *drugs*. The word was still in use as a form of 'drudges'.

MASTER GALLIPOT

Ha, ha, 'tis such a wasp; it does me good now to have her
sting me, little rogue.

MISTRESS GALLIPOT

Now fie how you vex me, I cannot abide these apron   30
husbands: such cotqueans, you overdo your things, they become you scurvily.

MASTER GALLIPOT

[*Aside*] Upon my life she breeds, heaven knows how I have
strained myself to please her, night and day: I wonder why
we citizens should get children so fretful and untoward in the   35
breeding, their fathers being for the most part as gentle as
milch kine.—Shall I leave thee, my Pru?

MISTRESS GALLIPOT

Fie, fie, fie.

MASTER GALLIPOT

Thou shalt not be vexed no more, pretty kind rogue, take no
cold, sweet Pru.   40

                                        Exit MASTER GALLIPOT

MISTRESS GALLIPOT

As your wit has done. Now Master Laxton, show your head,
what news from you? Would any husband suspect that a
woman crying 'Buy any scurvy-grass' should bring love
letters amongst her herbs to his wife? Pretty trick, fine convey-
ance: had jealousy a thousand eyes, a silly woman with   45
scurvy-grass blinds them all;
Laxton, with bays
Crown I thy wit for this, it deserves praise.
This makes me affect thee more, this proves thee wise,
'Lack, what poor shift is love forced to devise!   50
—To th' point.   *She reads the letter*
'Oh sweet creature—' (a sweet beginning) 'pardon my long
absence, for thou shalt shortly be possessed with my pres-

---

29 *sting* ed. (sing Q); arouse sexually (and cf. *The Taming of the
     Shrew*, II.i, 213f.)
30 *apron husbands* (aperne Q) husbands who follow their wives as if
     tied to their apron strings (Collier)
43 *scurvy-grass* coclearia officinalis, thought to be anti-scorbutic

---

31 *cotqueans.* Used contemptuously of men who act the housewife and
     meddle in the women's province; Bullen's view that the word is a
     variant form of 'cock-quean' or 'cuckquean' (a female cuckold) seems
     unacceptable, and, unusually, no sexual quibble seems intended.

ence; though Demophon was false to Phyllis, I will be to thee
as Pan-da-rus was to Cres-sida: though Aeneas made an ass   55
of Dido, I will die to thee ere I do so; oh sweetest creature,
make much of me, for no man beneath the silver moon shall
make more of a woman than I do of thee: furnish me therefore with thirty pounds, you must do it of necessity for me; I
languish till I see some comfort come from thee; protesting   60
not to die in thy debt, but rather to live so, as hitherto I have
and will,
                                        Thy true Laxton ever'.
Alas poor gentleman, troth I pity him,
How shall I raise this money? thirty pound?   65
'Tis thirty sure, a 3 before an 0,
I know his threes too well. My childbed linen?
Shall I pawn that for him? then if my mark
Be known I am undone; it may be thought
My husband's bankrupt: which way shall I turn?   70
Laxton, what with my own fears, and thy wants,
I'm like a needle 'twixt two adamants.

                    Enter MASTER GALLIPOT *hastily*

MASTER GALLIPOT
Nay, nay, wife, the women are all up. [*Aside*] Ha, how, read-
ing o' letters? I smell a goose, a couple of capons, and a gam-
mon of bacon from her mother out of the country, I hold my   75
life.
—Steal, steal—
MISTRESS GALLIPOT Oh beshrew your heart.
MASTER GALLIPOT   What letter's that?
    I'll see't.   *She tears the letter*
MISTRESS GALLIPOT Oh would thou hadst no eyes to see
The downfall of me and thyself: I'm forever,
Forever I'm undone.

56 *die to thee* punning on the sense of spend sexually
72 *adamants* loadstones or magnets
75 *I hold my life* by my life, I'm sure of it
77 lineation ed. (prose Q)

54 *Demophon.* Son of Theseus: Phyllis, a princess of Thrace, hanged
    herself when he failed to keep his promise to return to her; she was
    turned into an almond tree which bore leaves when Demophon came at
    last and embraced it.
55 *Pan-da-rus . . . Cres-sida.* So in Q, 'to mark the difficulty with which
    such hard names were read by Mistress Gallipot' (Dyce).

MASTER GALLIPOT   What ails my Pru?   80
  What paper's that thou tear'st?
MISTRESS GALLIPOT   Would I could tear
  My very heart in pieces: for my soul
  Lies on the rack of shame, that tortures me
  Beyond a woman's suffering.
MASTER GALLIPOT   What means this?
MISTRESS GALLIPOT
  Had you no other vengeance to throw down,   85
  But even in height of all my joys—
MASTER GALLIPOT   Dear woman—
MISTRESS GALLIPOT
  When the full sea of pleasure and content
  Seemed to flow over me—
MASTER GALLIPOT   As thou desirest
  To keep me out of bedlam, tell what troubles thee,
  Is not thy child at nurse fallen sick, or dead?   90
MISTRESS GALLIPOT
  Oh no.
MASTER GALLIPOT Heavens bless me, are my barns and houses
  Yonder at Hockley Hole consumed with fire?
  I can build more, sweet Pru.
MISTRESS GALLIPOT   'Tis worse, 'tis worse.
MASTER GALLIPOT
  My factor broke? or is the Jonas sunk?
MISTRESS GALLIPOT
  Would all we had were swallowed in the waves,   95
  Rather than both should be the scorn of slaves.
MASTER GALLIPOT
  I'm at my wits' end.
MISTRESS GALLIPOT   Oh my dear husband,

---

90 *at nurse* lodged away from home with a wet-nurse
94 *broke* absconded (or possibly bankrupt)

---

92 *Hockley Hole.* Hockley-in-the-Hole was later infamous as the resort of
  thieves and highwaymen, but also a place of amusement: it lay at the
  centre of what is now Clerkenwell. So notorious was it that in 1774 it
  was thought fitting formally to remove its name from the map, and it
  became Ray Street. Until the late 18th century Cold Bath Fields were
  immediately adjacent to the west.

Where once I thought myself a fixed star,
Placed only in the heaven of thine arms,
I fear now I shall prove a wanderer;   100
Oh Laxton, Laxton, is it then my fate
To be by thee o'erthrown?

MASTER GALLIPOT   Defend me, wisdom,
From falling into frenzy. On my knees,
Sweet Pru, speak, what's that Laxton who so heavy
Lies on thy bosom?

MISTRESS GALLIPOT   I shall sure run mad.   105

MASTER GALLIPOT
I shall run mad for company then: speak to me,
I'm Gallipot thy husband,—Pru,—why Pru,
Art sick in conscience for some villainous deed
Thou wert about to act? didst mean to rob me?
Tush I forgive thee; hast thou on my bed   110
Thrust my soft pillow under another's head?
I'll wink at all faults, Pru, 'las, that's no more
Than what some neighbours near thee have done before:
Sweet honey Pru, what's that Laxton?

MISTRESS GALLIPOT   Oh.

MASTER GALLIPOT
Out with him.

MISTRESS GALLIPOT Oh he's born to be my undoer.   115
This hand which thou call'st thine, to him was given,
To him was I made sure i'th'sight of heaven.

MASTER GALLIPOT
I never heard this thunder.

MISTRESS GALLIPOT   Yes, yes, before
I was to thee contracted, to him I swore:

---

118 *thunder* menace

98 *a fixed star.* See note to I.ii, 134, and cf. Shakespeare, Sonnet CXVI:
  'love ... is an ever-fixed mark, ... the star to every wandering bark'.
  'Wanderer' here only loosely suggests the movement of a meteor, and
  rather refers to Mistress Gallipot's simulated fear that she may prove
  loose.

117 *made sure.* Contracted, betrothed: she is inventing a contract *de praesenti*,
  sworn before witnesses and a canonical impediment to any future
  marriage to another. cf. *A Chaste Maid*, IV.i, 227, and *A Trick to Catch
  the Old One*, IV.iv, 92, in which play there is a scene closely similar to
  this one.

Since last I saw him, twelve months three times told   120
The moon hath drawn through her light silver bow,
For o'er the seas he went, and it was said
(But rumour lies) that he in France was dead.
But he's alive, oh he's alive, he sent
That letter to me, which in rage I rent,   125
Swearing with oaths most damnably to have me,
Or tear me from this bosom: oh heavens save me.

MASTER GALLIPOT
My heart will break,—shamed and undone forever.

MISTRESS GALLIPOT
So black a day, poor wretch, went o'er thee never.

MASTER GALLIPOT
If thou should'st wrestle with him at the law,   130
Th'art sure to fall, no odd sleight, no prevention.
I'll tell him th'art with child.

MISTRESS GALLIPOT   Hm.

MASTER GALLIPOT   Or give out
One of my men was ta'en abed with thee.

MISTRESS GALLIPOT
Hm, hm.

MASTER GALLIPOT Before I lose thee, my dear Pru,
I'll drive it to that push.

MISTRESS GALLIPOT   Worse, and worse still,   135
You embrace a mischief, to prevent an ill.

MASTER GALLIPOT
I'll buy thee of him, stop his mouth with gold,
Think'st thou 'twill do?

MISTRESS GALLIPOT   Oh me, heavens grant it would;
Yet now my senses are set more in tune,
He writ, as I remember in his letter,   140
That he in riding up and down had spent,
Ere he could find me, thirty pounds, send that,
Stand not on thirty with him.

MASTER GALLIPOT   Forty, Pru,
Say thou the word, 'tis done: we venture lives
For wealth, but must do more to keep our wives: 145

131 *no odd sleight* (slight Q—a frequent spelling) no cunning device to
      prevent her being overcome

120-1 Mistress Gallipot sees herself momentarily as the Empress of Babylon,
      whose speech about the Fairy Queen in *The Whore of Babylon* (I.i,
      46ff.) she half-remembers: 'Five summers have scarce drawn their
      glimmering nights/Through the moon's silver bow . . .'

Thirty or forty, Pru?

MISTRESS GALLIPOT   Thirty, good sweet;
Of an ill bargain let's save what we can,
I'll pay it him with my tears, he was a man
When first I knew him of a meek spirit,
All goodness is not yet dried up I hope.   150

MASTER GALLIPOT
He shall have thirty pound, let that stop all:
Love's sweets taste best, when we have drunk down gall.

Enter MASTER TILTYARD, *and his wife,* MASTER GOSHAWK *and*
MISTRESS OPENWORK

God-so, our friends; come, come, smooth your cheek;
After a storm the face of heaven looks sleek.

MASTER TILTYARD
Did I not tell you these turtles were together?   155

MISTRESS TILTYARD
How dost thou, sirrah? why, sister Gallipot!

MISTRESS OPENWORK
Lord, how she's changed!

GOSHAWK
Is your wife ill, sir?

MASTER GALLIPOT
Yes indeed, la sir, very ill, very ill, never worse.

MISTRESS TILTYARD
How her head burns, feel how her pulses work.   160

MISTRESS OPENWORK
Sister, lie down a little, that always does me good.

MISTRESS TILTYARD
In good sadness, I find best ease in that too; has she laid
some hot thing to her stomach?

MISTRESS GALLIPOT
No, but I will lay something anon.

MASTER TILTYARD
Come, come fools, you trouble her, shall's go, Master   165
Goshawk?

GOSHAWK
Yes, sweet Master Tiltyard.—Sirrah Rosamond, I hold my
life Gallipot hath vexed his wife.

153 *God-so* said to be a variant form of 'catso', an **exclamation** of
    surprise or alarm
156 *sirrah* frequently feminine
162 *sadness* seriousness

MISTRESS OPENWORK
She has a horrible high colour indeed.

GOSHAWK
We shall have your face painted with the same red soon at 170
night, when your husband comes from his rubbers in a false
alley; thou wilt not believe me that his bowls run with a
wrong bias.

MISTRESS OPENWORK
It cannot sink into me, that he feeds upon stale mutton
abroad, having better and fresher at home. 175

GOSHAWK
What if I bring thee where thou shalt see him stand at rack
and manger?

MISTRESS OPENWORK
I'll saddle him in's kind, and spur him till he kick again.

GOSHAWK
Shall thou and I ride our journey then?

MISTRESS OPENWORK
Here's my hand. 180

GOSHAWK
No more; come, Master Tiltyard, shall we leap into the

---

174 *feeds . . . abroad* a common phrase for marital unfaithfulness
174 *mutton* food for lust, hence prostitutes
178 *saddle him in's kind* use him according to the man he is, do by
him as he does by me (picking up Goshawk's submerged metaphor)
179 *ride our journey* enjoy our sexual pleasure

171–2 *his rubbers in a false alley.* Bowls was an exceedingly popular game at
this period: the alleys were often the scene of gambling and dissipation
which numerous acts of Parliament failed to curb. cf. Stephen Gosson,
School of Abuse (1579): 'common bowling alleys are privy moths, that
eat up the credit of many idle citizens, whose gains at home are not
able to weigh down their losses abroad, whose shops are so far from
maintaining their play, that wives and children cry out for bread, and
go to bed supperless oft in the year' (*Sh. Eng.*, II, 465). *Rubbers* was
often a singular form. To bowl out the rubbers 'is to bowl a third game
for the bets, when the players have gotten one apiece' (Randle Holme,
Academy of Armoury, 1688). Rubbing has also a sexual meaning:
cf. *Love's Labour's Lost*, IV.i, 139–40 where Costard says 'She's too
hard for you at pricks sir, challenge her to bowl' and Boyet replies 'I
fear too much rubbing'.
176–7 *at rack and manger.* sc. at his 'food'. To live at rack and manger was
to live in reckless abundance. cf. Wyclif, *Works*, 435 (qu. *Oxf. Dict.
English Proverbs*, 661): 'it is yuel to kepe a wast hors in stable . . . but it
is worse to have a woman at racke and at manger'.

stirrups with our women, and amble home?

MASTER TILTYARD

Yes, yes, come wife.

MISTRESS TILTYARD

In troth sister, I hope you will do well for all this.

MISTRESS GALLIPOT

I hope I shall: farewell good sister: sweet Master Goshawk. 185

MASTER GALLIPOT

Welcome brother, most kindly welcome sir.

OMNES

Thanks, sir, for our good cheer.

         Exeunt all but GALLIPOT *and his wife*

MASTER GALLIPOT

 It shall be so; because a crafty knave

 Shall not outreach me, nor walk by my door

 With my wife arm in arm, as 'twere his whore,   190

 I'll give him a golden coxcomb; thirty pound,

 Tush Pru, what's thirty pound? sweet duck, look cheerly.

MISTRESS GALLIPOT

 Thou art worthy of my heart, thou buy'st it dearly.

        Enter LAXTON *muffled*

LAXTON

Uds light, the tide's against me, a pox of your pothecaryship: oh for some glister to set him going; 'tis one of Hercules' 195 labours to tread one of these city hens, because their cocks are still crowing over them; there's no turning tail here, I must on.

MISTRESS GALLIPOT

Oh husband see, he comes.

MASTER GALLIPOT

Let me deal with him.   200

LAXTON

Bless you, sir.

MASTER GALLIPOT

Be you blest too, sir, if you come in peace.

---

188 *because* to the end that
197 *still* always

---

182 *amble.* Originally used only of horses; the whole sentence continues the sexual punning.
195 *glister.* An old form of 'clyster', an enema. The word was used contemptuously of doctors and apothecaries (as in the character name of the quack in *A Family of Love*).

LAXTON
  Have you any good pudding tobacco, sir?
MISTRESS GALLIPOT
  Oh pick no quarrels, gentle sir, my husband
  Is not a man of weapon, as you are,   205
  He knows all, I have opened all before him
  Concerning you.
LAXTON   Zounds, has she shown my letters?
MISTRESS GALLIPOT
  Suppose my case were yours, what would you do
  At such a pinch, such batteries, such assaults,
  Of father, mother, kindred, to dissolve   210
  The knot you tied, and to be bound to him?
  How could you shift this storm off?
LAXTON   If I know, hang me.
MISTRESS GALLIPOT
  Besides, a story of your death was read
  Each minute to me.
LAXTON [*Aside*]   What a pox means this riddling?
MASTER GALLIPOT
  Be wise, sir, let not you and I be tossed   215
  On lawyers' pens; they have sharp nibs and draw
  Men's very heart-blood from them; what need you, sir,
  To beat the drum of my wife's infamy,
  And call your friends together, sir, to prove
  Your precontract, when sh'has confessed it?
LAXTON   Hm sir,   220
  Has she confessed it?
MASTER GALLIPOT   Sh'has, faith, to me, sir,
  Upon your letter sending.
MISTRESS GALLIPOT   I have, I have.
LAXTON
  [*Aside*] If I let this iron cool, call me slave.
  —Do you hear, you dame Prudence? think'st thou, vile
  woman,   225
  I'll take these blows and wink?
MISTRESS GALLIPOT   Upon my knees—

215 *tossed* bandied, made the subject of talk
220 *precontract* ed. (precontact Q) cf. above, l. 118n.

203 *pudding tobacco.* Compressed tobacco made into rolls resembling a
  pudding or sausage; but the threat in Laxton's words which Mistress
  Gallipot recognizes probably comes from the suggestion that he is after
  Gallipot's pudding or guts.

LAXTON
  Out, impudence.
MASTER GALLIPOT   Good sir—
LAXTON   You goatish slaves,
  No wild fowl to cut up but mine?
MASTER GALLIPOT   Alas sir,
  You make her flesh to tremble: fright her not,
  She shall do reason, and what's fit.
LAXTON   I'll have thee,   230
  Wert thou more common than an hospital,
  And more diseased.
MASTER GALLIPOT   But one word, good sir.
LAXTON   So, sir.
MASTER GALLIPOT
  I married her, have lien with her, and got
  Two children on her body, think but on that;
  Have you so beggarly an appetite   235
  When I upon a dainty dish have fed
  To dine upon my scraps, my leavings? ha, sir?
  Do I come near you now, sir?
LAXTON   Be-Lady, you touch me.
MASTER GALLIPOT
  Would not you scorn to wear my clothes, sir?
LAXTON   Right, sir.
MASTER GALLIPOT
  Then pray, sir, wear not her, for she's a garment   240
  So fitting for my body I'm loath
  Another should put it on, you will undo both.
  Your letter (as she said) complained you had spent
  In quest of her some thirty pound, I'll pay it;
  Shall that, sir, stop this gap up 'twixt you two?   245
LAXTON
  Well, if I swallow this wrong, let her thank you:
  The money being paid, sir, I am gone;

231 *common* open to all comers; cf. III.i, 135
236 *a dainty dish* cf. the modern slang 'dish' for an attractive girl
238 *now* ed. (uow Q)
238 *Be-Lady* a corruption of 'By our Lady'

228 ' "To cut up wild fowl" was a cant expression, the meaning of which is
    sufficiently obvious' (Bullen). It seems, however, not to be recorded in
    OED or in contemporary canting dictionaries. But cf. Webster, *The
    White Devil*, II.i, 90–2: 'We fear/When Tiber to each prowling pas-
    senger/Discovers flocks of wild ducks . . .' and *Cymbeline*, I.iv, 88:
    'strange fowl light upon neighbouring ponds'.

Farewell: oh women! happy's he trusts none.
MISTRESS GALLIPOT
Despatch him hence, sweet husband.
MASTER GALLIPOT   Yes, dear wife:
Pray sir, come in: ere Master Laxton part   250
Thou shalt in wine drink to him.
MISTRESS GALLIPOT   With all my heart.

Exit MASTER GALLIPOT

—How dost thou like my wit?
LAXTON   Rarely: that wile
By which the serpent did the first woman beguile
Did ever since all women's bosoms fill;
Y'are apple-eaters all, deceivers still.   [*Exeunt*]   255

[Act III, Scene iii]

Enter SIR ALEXANDER WENGRAVE, SIR DAVY DAPPER, SIR ADAM
APPLETON *at one door, and* TRAPDOOR *at another door*

SIR ALEXANDER
Out with your tale, Sir Davy, to Sir Adam:
A knave is in mine eye deep in my debt.
SIR DAVY
Nay: if he be a knave, sir, hold him fast.

[SIR DAVY *and* SIR ADAM *talk apart*]

SIR ALEXANDER
Speak softly, what egg is there hatching now?
TRAPDOOR
A duck's egg, sir, a duck that has eaten a frog. I have cracked   5
the shell, and some villainy or other will peep out presently;
the duck that sits is the bouncing ramp, that roaring girl my
mistress, the drake that must tread is your son Sebastian.

251 s.d. *Exit* MASTER GALLIPOT ed. (Exit Maister Gallipot and his
     wife Q)
255 s.d. *Exeunt* ed. (Exit Laxton Q)
   2 *A knave . . . debt* i.e., I have caught sight of a knave who is in my
     debt
   7 *bouncing ramp* rampant, wanton creature

s.d. *at one door . . . at another.* i.e., of the stage: the setting is in fact a
     street.
   5 *a duck that has eaten a frog.* The phrase seems to have no more specific
     meaning than an allusion to the villainy that Trapdoor goes on to speak
     about.

SIR ALEXANDER
  Be quick.
TRAPDOOR
  As the tongue of an oyster-wench.   10
SIR ALEXANDER
  And see thy news be true.
TRAPDOOR
  As a barber's every Saturday night. Mad Moll—
SIR ALEXANDER
  Ah.
TRAPDOOR
  Must be let in without knocking at your back gate.
SIR ALEXANDER
  So.   15
TRAPDOOR
  Your chamber will be made bawdy.
SIR ALEXANDER
  Good.
TRAPDOOR
  She comes in a shirt of mail.
SIR ALEXANDER
  How, shirt of mail?
TRAPDOOR
  Yes sir, or a male shirt, that's to say in man's apparel.   20
SIR ALEXANDER
  To my son?
TRAPDOOR
  Close to your son: your son and her moon will be in con-
  junction, if all almanacs lie not: her black saveguard is turned
  into a deep slop, the holes of her upper body to button-

---

23 *saveguard* see II.i, 158
24 *slop* see II.ii, 79 and n.

---

12 *As a barber's every Saturday night.* Presumably so that he can go to
    church on Sunday with a good conscience.
22–3 *in conjunction.* Two planets were said to be in conjunction when they
    were in the same sign of the zodiac (their influences were then thought
    to reinforce one another); the moon is in conjunction with the sun at
    new moon. But 'conjunction' was also commonly used for copulation.
24 *holes of her upper body.* 'Hole' has various low sexual uses and here
    possibly suggests nipples. But 'body' (of which 'bodice' is a variant
    form of the plural) was regularly used for the part of a woman's dress
    above the waist, which would commonly be laced through a series of
    holes. cf. *A Mad World, My Masters,* III.iii, 100.

holes, her waistcoat to a doublet, her placket to the ancient   25
seat of a codpiece, and you shall take 'em both with standing
collars.

SIR ALEXANDER
Art sure of this?

TRAPDOOR
As every throng is sure of a pickpocket, as sure as a whore is
of the clients all Michaelmas Term, and of the pox after the   30
term.

SIR ALEXANDER
The time of their tilting?

TRAPDOOR
Three.

SIR ALEXANDER
The day?

TRAPDOOR
This.   35

SIR ALEXANDER
Away, ply it, watch her.

TRAPDOOR
As the devil doth for the death of a bawd, I'll watch her,
do you catch her.

SIR ALEXANDER
She's fast: here weave thou the nets, hark.

TRAPDOOR
They are made.   40

SIR ALEXANDER
I told them thou didst owe me money; hold it up: maintain't.

TRAPDOOR
Stiffly, as a puritan does contention;—pox, I owe thee not

---

25 *placket* the opening or slit at the top of a skirt or petticoat (con-
    stantly, like 'codpiece', with sexual associations)
41 *them* sc. the other knights
41 *hold it up* sc. the pretence
42 *pox* ed. (Foxe Q)

---

25 *waistcoat.* In the sixteenth and early seventeenth centuries elaborate
    waistcoats were fashionable. They were worn beneath an outer gown,
    but so as to be seen.
26–7 *standing collars.* Upstanding collars became fashionable for men in
    the early seventeenth century: see the illustration on the title-page.
    There is probably a play on 'stand' in the sense of an erection (cf. I.ii,
    56n.) and conceivably a hint of some contraceptive device.
30 *Michaelmas Term.* The first term of the legal year, when the termers will
    have plenty of money.

the value of a halfpenny halter.   [*Angrily, as in a quarrel*]

SIR ALEXANDER

Thou shalt be hanged in't ere thou scape so. Varlet, I'll
make thee look through a grate.   45

TRAPDOOR

I'll do't presently, through a tavern grate. Drawer! Pish.

Exit TRAPDOOR

SIR ADAM

Has the knave vexed you, sir?

SIR ALEXANDER   Asked him my money,
He swears my son received it: oh that boy
Will ne'er leave heaping sorrows on my heart,
Till he has broke it quite.

SIR ADAM   Is he still wild?   50

SIR ALEXANDER

As is a Russian bear.

SIR ADAM   But he has left
His old haunt with that baggage?

SIR ALEXANDER   Worse still and worse,
He lays on me his shame, I on him my curse.

SIR DAVY

My son Jack Dapper then shall run with him,
All in one pasture.

SIR ADAM   Proves your son bad too, sir?   55

SIR DAVY

As villainy can make him: your Sebastian
Doats but on one drab, mine on a thousand,
A noise of fiddlers, tobacco, wine and a whore,
A mercer that will let him take up more,
Dice, and a water-spaniel with a duck: oh,   60
Bring him abed with these, when his purse jingles,
Roaring boys follow at's tail, fencers and ningles
(Beasts Adam ne'er gave name to), these horse-leeches suck

45 *grate* prison grating
58 *noise* band of musicians (not necessarily contemptuously)
59 *take up* sc. on credit
62 *ningles* (or ingles) boy-favourites, catamites
63 *horse-leeches* farriers (alternatively a large variety of leech), widely
    used as a contemptuous term for rapacious parasites: cf. *A Fair
    Quarrel*, III.ii, 170

46 *Drawer!* He calls offstage as to a drawer in the tavern.
51 *Russian bear*. cf. Macbeth, III.iv, 99 ('the rugged Russian bear'). Bears
    were imported from Russia for baiting, and their fierceness became
    proverbial.

My son: he being drawn dry, they all live on smoke.
SIR ALEXANDER
    Tobacco?
SIR DAVY   Right: but I have in my brain   65
    A windmill going that shall grind to dust
    The follies of my son, and make him wise,
    Or a stark fool; pray lend me your advice.
BOTH
    That shall you, good Sir Davy.
SIR DAVY   Here's the springe
    I ha' set to catch this woodcock in: an action   70
    In a false name (unknown to him) is entered
    I'th'counter to arrest Jack Dapper.
BOTH   Ha, ha, he.
SIR DAVY
    Think you the counter cannot break him?
SIR ADAM   Break him?
    Yes and break's heart too if he lie there long.
SIR DAVY
    I'll make him sing a counter-tenor sure.   75
SIR ADAM
    No way to tame him like it, there he shall learn
    What money is indeed, and how to spend it.
SIR DAVY
    He's bridled there.
SIR ALEXANDER   Ay, yet knows not how to mend it:
    Bedlam cures not more madmen in a year
    Than one of the counters does: men pay more dear   80
    There for their wit than anywhere; a counter,

---

72 *counter* the mayor's court or hall of justice, to which a **debtor's**
   prison was attached; also written 'compter'

---

65 *Tobacco.* The popularity of smoking by the early years of James I's
   reign is evidenced by Barnabe Riche's estimate that there were then at
   least seven thousand tobacco shops in London: annual takings were
   said to be over £300,000.
66 *windmill.* Picking up the implied image of a tobacco-mill.
68 *advice* ed. (advise Q). Q spelling gives a perfect rhyme.
69–70 *the springe . . . to catch this woodcock.* Probably a direct theft from
   Hamlet, I.iv, 115, which seems to be the first recorded instance of the
   figurative use of this phrase, though 'woodcock' was in common use for
   simpleton. cf also *Twelfth Night*, II.v, 84.
78 *bridled.* With a quibble on Bridewell, already a common term for a
   house of correction.

Why 'tis an university, who not sees?
As scholars there, so here men take degrees,
And follow the same studies all alike.
Scholars learn first logic and rhetoric,   85
So does a prisoner; with fine honey'd speech
At's first coming in he doth persuade, beseech
He may be lodged with one that is not itchy,
To lie in a clean chamber, in sheets not lousy;
But when he has no money, then does he try   90
By subtle logic and quaint sophistry
To make the keepers trust him.

SIR ADAM   Say they do?
SIR ALEXANDER
Then he's a graduate.
SIR DAVY   Say they trust him not?
SIR ALEXANDER
Then is he held a freshman and a sot,
And never shall commence, but, being still barred,   95
Be expulsed from the master's side, to th' twopenny ward,
Or else i'th'Hole beg place.
SIR ADAM   When then, I pray,
Proceeds a prisoner?
SIR ALEXANDER   When, money being the theme,

95 *commence* be admitted to a degree
98 *Proceeds* advance from B.A. to a higher degree

---

82 *an university.* Middleton was fond of this joke. cf. *The Phoenix*, IV.iii, 19
and *Michaelmas Term*, III.iv, 83ff.: 'H'as at least sixteen at this instant
proceeded in both the Counters: some bach'lors, some masters, some
doctors of captivity'. Sir Thomas Overbury in 1613 called a prison 'an
university of poor scholars, in which three arts are chiefly studied; to
pray, to curse, and to write letters'. The joke survived until the nine-
teenth century when the Marshalsea was still known as the college,
as in *Little Dorrit*.

85 *logic and rhetoric.* From the foundation of the universities logic was
regarded as the science of sciences, and both these subjects held a
principal place in the curricula of the English universities until the
middle of the seventeenth century.

96 *the master's side.* The governor of a prison was allowed to let certain
rooms for his own profit; these were, of course, the best in the prison.
The twopenny ward (cf. Chapman, etc., *Eastward Ho!*, V.ii, 61) may be
the mistress's side referred to in *The Phoenix* (IV.iii, 22). The poorest
prisoners were confined in *the Hole*, a name specially given to the worst
dungeon in the Wood Street Counter.

97 *beg place.* ed. (beg plac't Q) Perhaps, with previous editors, we should
read 'be placed', but the chosen reading has a nice irony.

He can dispute with his hard creditors' hearts,
And get out clear, he's then a Master of Arts.
Sir Davy, send your son to Wood Street College,
A gentleman can nowhere get more knowledge.

SIR DAVY

There gallants study hard.

SIR ALEXANDER　　　　　　　　True: to get money.

SIR DAVY

'Lies by th' heels i'faith: thanks, thanks, I ha' sent
For a couple of bears shall paw him.

Enter SERGEANT CURTILAX *and* YEOMAN HANGER

SIR ADAM　　　　　　　　　　　　Who comes yonder?　　105

SIR DAVY

They look like puttocks, these should be they.

SIR ALEXANDER　　　　　　　　　　　　I know 'em,

They are officers: sir, we'll leave you.

SIR DAVY　　　　　　　　　　　　My good knights,

Leave me, you see I'm haunted now with spirits.

BOTH

Fare you well, sir.　　*Exeunt* [SIR] ALEX[ANDER] *and* [SIR] ADAM

CURTILAX

This old muzzle-chops should be he by the fellow's descrip-　110
tion:—save you, sir.

SIR DAVY

Come hither, you mad varlets, did not my man tell you I
watched here for you?

---

104 *'Lies by th' heels* (i.e., he lies) he is being arrested (or put in irons)
105 *bears* rough fellows: cf. 'boys more tough than bears' (*The Honest Whore*, part 1, IV.iii, 99)
106 *puttocks* kites, applied opprobriously to catchpolls
108 *spirits* kidnappers or abductors, with of course a play on the common sense

---

99 *dispute.* One proved one's right to proceed by engaging in a *disputatio*, in which parties formally sustain, attack, or defend a given question or thesis. There is a brief parody of a disputation in *A Chaste Maid in Cheapside*, IV.i.
101 *Wood Street College* (cf. above, l.82). Conditions in Wood Street Counter, which stood on the east side of the street near the junction with Gresham Street, seem to have been particularly bad even by the standards of the early seventeenth century (cf. *Sh. Eng.*, II, 508).

CURTILAX

One in a blue coat, sir, told us, that in this place an old
gentleman would watch for us, a thing contrary to our oath,   115
for we are to watch for every wicked member in a city.

SIR DAVY

You'll watch then for ten thousand, what's thy name
honestly?

CURTILAX

Sergeant Curtilax I, sir.

SIR DAVY

An excellent name for a sergeant, Curtilax.   120
Sergeants indeed are weapons of the law:
When prodigal ruffians far in debt are grown,
Should not you cut them, citizens were o'erthrown.
Thou dwell'st hereby in Holborn, Curtilax?

CURTILAX

That's my circuit, sir, I conjure most in that circle.   125

SIR DAVY

And what young toward whelp is this?

HANGER

Of the same litter, his yeoman, sir, my name's Hanger.

SIR DAVY

Yeoman Hanger:
One pair of shears sure cut out both your coats,
You have two names most dangerous to men's throats,   130
You two are villainous loads on gentlemen's backs,
Dear ware, this Hanger and this Curtilax.

126 *toward* promising, hopeful
127 *yeoman* an assistant to an official, but also a servant subordinate
    to a sergeant

---

114 *One in a blue coat*. This was then the traditional dress of a servant until
    the early seventeenth century.
118 *honestly* ed. (honesty Q). But 'honesty' was occasionally used as a collec-
    tive term for the gentry, and it is possible that this is an ironic use in the
    singular.
120 *Curtilax*. A much perverted form of 'cutlass', which became so distinct
    that it acquired a kind of permanent standing, the identification of the
    final part with 'ax' being favoured by the use of the weapon in delivering
    slashing blows (*OED*).
129 *One pair of shears . . . cut out both your coats*. i.e., you are two of a kind.
    'There went but a pair of shears between them' was a common prover-
    bial expression: cf. *Measure for Measure*, I.ii, 26.
132 *ware*. The word was sometimes used for textiles; the image is hardly
    precise.

CURTILAX
 We are as other men are, sir, I cannot see but he who makes
 a show of honesty and religion, if his claws can fasten to his
 liking, he draws blood; all that live in the world are but great   135
 fish and little fish, and feed upon one another, some eat up
 whole men, a sergeant cares but for the shoulder of a man;
 they call us knaves and curs, but many times he that sets us on
 worries more lambs one year than we do in seven.

SIR DAVY
 Spoke like a noble Cerberus: is the action entered?   140

HANGER
 His name is entered in the book of unbelievers.

SIR DAVY
 What book's that?

CURTILAX
 The book where all prisoners' names stand, and not one
 amongst forty, when he comes in, believes to come out in
 haste.   145

SIR DAVY
 Be as dogged to him as your office allows you to be.

BOTH
 Oh sir.

SIR DAVY
 You know the unthrift Jack Dapper?

CURTILAX
 Ay, ay, sir, that gull? as well as I know my yeoman.

SIR DAVY
 And you know his father too, Sir Davy Dapper?   150

CURTILAX
 As damned a usurer as ever was among Jews; if he were sure
 his father's skin would yield him any money, he would when

---

140 *Cerberus* watchdog

135–6 *great fish and little fish.* 'The great fish eat up the small' was a bitter
    proverbial jest of constant application. cf. *Pericles*, II.i, 27: 'Master, I
    marvel how the fishes live in the sea.—Why, as men do a-land; the
    great ones eat up the little ones'.
137 *for the shoulder of a man.* Because he apprehends men by catching hold
    of their shoulders.

he dies flay it off, and sell it to cover drums for children at
Bartholomew Fair.

SIR DAVY

[*Aside*] What toads are these to spit poison on a man to his   155
face!—Do you see, my honest rascals? yonder greyhound is
the dog he hunts with, out of that tavern Jack Dapper will
sally: sa, sa; give the counter, on, set upon him.

BOTH

We'll charge him upo'th'back, sir.

SIR DAVY

Take no bail, put mace enough into his caudle, double your   160
files, traverse your ground.

BOTH

Brave, sir.

SIR DAVY

Cry arm, arm, arm.

BOTH

Thus, sir.

SIR DAVY

There boy, there boy, away: look to your prey, my true   165
English wolves, and so I vanish.   *Exit* SIR DAVY

CURTILAX

Some warden of the sergeants begat this old fellow, upon
my life: stand close.

153 flay ed. (flea Q)
158 *sa, sa* in hunting, a call to attention
166 *and* ed. (and and Q)
167 *Some warden of the sergeants* one, that is, crabbed enough to be in
charge of sergeants

---

154 *Bartholomew Fair* had by this time grown to enormous size, incorpora-
ting four parishes and lasting for a fortnight from 23 August (St Bartholomew's Eve), when it was opened by the Lord Mayor. It was the
Londoner's great annual jamboree, and, amongst other things, the chief
national cloth sale.
158 *give the counter*. To hunt counter is to run a false scent, or follow it in
reverse direction; so here, turn him back. There is doubtless a play on
counter in the sense of prison (cf. above, ll. 72ff.).
160 *mace*. Sergeants carried maces; *caudle* is gruel mixed with spiced ale, for
which mace would be a regular ingredient. The same jest appears in
A Mad World, My Masters, III.ii, 69.
160-1 *double your files, traverse your ground*. Literally, make the ranks smaller
by putting two files in one, move from side to side; but Sir Davy is
presumably just being briskly military, using at random the terms he
knows.

HANGER
Shall the ambuscado lie in one place?
CURTILAX
No, nook thou yonder.   170

Enter MOLL *and* TRAPDOOR

MOLL
Ralph.
TRAPDOOR
What says my brave captain male and female?
MOLL
This Holborn is such a wrangling street.
TRAPDOOR
That's because lawyers walks to and fro in't.
MOLL
Here's such jostling, as if everyone we met were drunk and   175
reeled.
TRAPDOOR
Stand, mistress, do you not smell carrion?
MOLL
Carrion? no, yet I spy ravens.
TRAPDOOR
Some poor wind-shaken gallant will anon fall into sore
labour, and these men-midwives must bring him to bed i'the   180
counter, there all those that are great with child with debts
lie in.

169 *ambuscado* ambush, a common 17th-century form used especially
      of the force employed
170 *nook thou yonder* ed. (uooke Q) hide in that nook
173 *wrangling* noisy, disputatious
179 *wind-shaken* weakened or flawed at heart as timber supposed
      cracked by force of the wind

---

174 Several inns of court stood in Holborn, then as now the principal east-
      west street in the northern part of the City.
177 *carrion*. A carrion or carren doe was one which was pregnant (cf.
      Gascoigne, *Woodmanship*, 5): hence the quibbles in Trapdoor's next
      speech. Ravens are carrion-eaters (in the more familiar sense), but
      'raven' or 'ravin' also means robbery or rapine. The complex joke is now
      irrecoverable without much labour.
180 *men-midwives*. Another well-used joke. cf. *The Whore of Babylon*,
      II.i, 61ff.: 'Do you not know (mistress) what Sergeants are? . . . why
      they are certain men-midwives, that never bring people to bed, but
      when they are sore in labour, that nobody else can deliver them'. And
      see Jonson, *The Staple of News*, ind. 43ff. and Field, *Amends for Ladies*,
      IV.i, 164f.

MOLL
Stand up.

TRAPDOOR
Like your new maypole.

HANGER
Whist, whew.   185

CURTILAX
Hump, no.

MOLL
Peeping? it shall go hard, huntsmen, but I'll spoil your game: they look for all the world like two infected maltmen coming muffled up in their cloaks in a frosty morning to London.

TRAPDOOR
A course, captain; a bear comes to the stake.   190

Enter JACK DAPPER *and* GULL

MOLL
It should be so, for the dogs struggle to be let loose.

HANGER
Whew.

CURTILAX
Hemp.

MOLL
Hark Trapdoor, follow your leader.

JACK DAPPER
Gull.   195

GULL
Master.

JACK DAPPER
Didst ever see such an ass as I am, boy?

GULL
No by my troth, sir, to lose all your money, yet have false dice of your own, why 'tis as I saw a great fellow used t'other day,

---

185 *Whist* Hanger whistles questioningly to Curtilax; *whew* is like-
    wise a whistle, but also a verb meaning to move sharply
190 *course* encounter, passage at arms

---

188 *two infected maltmen.* Presumably the cloaks would hide the visible
    signs of an infection (but 'infected' could mean tainted with crime).
    I do not know why maltmen (or maltsters) should be picked on; but cf.
    No Wit, No Help, Like a Woman's, III.i, 53–4: 'Let each man look to
    his part now, and not feed/Upon one dish all four on's, like plain malt-
    men'. Maltmen appear in several proverbs, none of which seems to tell
    on the present context.

he had a fair sword and buckler, and yet a butcher dry-beat   200
him with a cudgel.

MOLL AND TRAPDOOR

Honest servant, fly; fly, Master Dapper, you'll be arrested
else.

JACK DAPPER

Run, Gull, and draw.

GULL

Run, master, Gull follows you.   205

Exit [JACK] DAPPER *and* GULL

CURTILAX

I know you well enough, you're but a whore to hang upon
any man.

MOLL

Whores then are like sergeants, so now hang you;—draw,
rogue, but strike not: for a broken pate they'll keep their
beds, and recover twenty marks damages.   210

CURTILAX

You shall pay for this rescue;—run down Shoe Lane and
meet him.

TRAPDOOR

Shoo, is this a rescue, gentlemen, or no?

MOLL

Rescue? a pox on 'em, Trapdoor, let's away,
I'm glad I have done perfect one good work today;   215
If any gentleman be in scrivener's bands,
Send but for Moll, she'll bail him by these hands.   *Exeunt*

200 *dry-beat* beat soundly (with 'dry blows', i.e., those not drawing
  blood)
202 s.p. MOLL AND TRAPDOOR ed. (Both Q): perhaps the speech should
  be divided between the two
209 *rogue* i.e., Trapdoor
210 *twenty marks* the mark was worth 13s. 4d.
216 *scrivener* in the general sense of notary

---

202 *servant* ed. (Serieant Q corr.; Seriant Q uncorr.) Q is plainly wrong, and
  I follow Dyce and Bullen. Bowers reads 'Sir' on the grounds that Gull
  would not be referred to before his master, and thinks the compositor
  may have mistakenly expanded the abbreviation 'Sʳ'. That would be an
  odd mistake; and who would call Jack Dapper 'Honest Sir'?
206 Bullen suggests that Moll holds Curtilax at this point.
211 *rescue.* The forcible taking of a person or goods out of custody—a very
  serious offence. cf. *Coriolanus*, III.i, 275, and *The Honest Whore*, part 1,
  IV.iii, 141: 'A rescue, prentices, my master's catchpolled'.
211 *Shoe Lane* (now bridged by Holborn Viaduct) ran down from Holborn
  towards Fleet Street and the Bridewell.

[Act IV, Scene i]

Enter SIR ALEXANDER WENGRAVE *solus*

SIR ALEXANDER

Unhappy in the follies of a son
Led against judgment, sense, obedience,
And all the powers of nobleness and wit;

Enter TRAPDOOR

Oh wretched father.—Now Trapdoor, will she come?

TRAPDOOR

In man's apparel, sir, I am in her heart now,   5
And share in all her secrets.

SIR ALEXANDER   Peace, peace, peace.

Here, take my German watch, hang't up in sight,
That I may see her hang in English for't.

TRAPDOOR

I warrant you for that now, next sessions rids her, sir,
this watch will bring her in better than a hundred con-   10
stables.

SIR ALEXANDER

Good Trapdoor, sayst thou so? thou cheer'st my heart
After a storm of sorrow,—my gold chain, too,
Here, take a hundred marks in yellow links.

TRAPDOOR

That will do well to bring the watch to light, sir: 15
And worth a thousand of your headborough's lanthorns.

SIR ALEXANDER

Place that o'the court cupboard, let it lie
Full in the view of her thief-whorish eye.

TRAPDOOR

She cannot miss it, sir, I see't so plain

16 *headborough* constable
17 *court cupboard* a form of sideboard consisting normally of three
shelves supported on elaborately carved legs

---

7 *my German watch.* Allusions to German watches and clocks are frequent in plays of this period. cf., e.g., *Love's Labour's Lost*, III.i, 87, and
A Mad World, My Masters, IV.i, 21. They were renowned for their
complexity and ingenuity.

14 *a hundred marks in yellow links.* sc. his chain of office as magistrate. Sir
Bounteous Progress is cheated of an identical one in *A Mad World,
My Masters* (V.i, 122 and V.ii, 170), where Follywit (disguised as a
player) asks for a chain to serve for a justice's hat.

That I could steal't myself.

SIR ALEXANDER   Perhaps thou shalt too,   20
  That or something as weighty; what she leaves,
  Thou shalt come closely in, and filch away,
  And all the weight upon her back I'll lay.

TRAPDOOR
  You cannot assure that, sir.

SIR ALEXANDER   No? what lets it?

TRAPDOOR
  Being a stout girl, perhaps she'll desire pressing,   25
  Then all the weight must lie upon her belly.

SIR ALEXANDER
  Belly or back I care not so I've one.

TRAPDOOR
  You're of my mind for that, sir.

SIR ALEXANDER
  Hang up my ruff-band with the diamond at it,
  It may be she'll like that best.   30

TRAPDOOR
  [*Aside*] It's well for her that she must have her choice, he
  thinks nothing too good for her.—If you hold on this mind a
  little longer, it shall be the first work I do to turn thief
  myself; would do a man good to be hanged when he is so
  well provided for.   35

SIR ALEXANDER
  So, well said; all hangs well, would she hung so too,
  The sight would please me more than all their glisterings:
  Oh that my mysteries to such straits should run,
  That I must rob myself to bless my son.   *Exeunt*

Enter SEBASTIAN, *with* MARY FITZ-ALLARD *like a page, and* MOLL
[in man's clothes]

SEBASTIAN
  Thou hast done me a kind office, without touch   40
  Either of sin or shame, our loves are honest.

MOLL
  I'd scorn to make such shift to bring you together else.

22 *closely* secretly
24 *lets* prevents
37 *glisterings* ed. (gilsterings Q)

---

38 *my mysteries* (stet Q). In the sense of cunning or craft. Dyce suggests
'miseries', but the mistake would be hard to account for, except through
the compositor's having two lines in his head and being influenced by
'glistering' (which he misspells). The Q reading can stand.

SEBASTIAN

Now have I time and opportunity
Without all fear to bid thee welcome, love.   *Kiss*

MARY

Never with more desire and harder venture.   45

MOLL

How strange this shows, one man to kiss another.

SEBASTIAN

I'd kiss such men to choose, Moll,
Methinks a woman's lip tastes well in a doublet.

MOLL

Many an old madam has the better fortune then,
Whose breaths grew stale before the fashion came: 50
If that will help 'em, as you think 'twill do,
They'll learn in time to pluck on the hose too.

SEBASTIAN

The older they wax, Moll (troth I speak seriously),
As some have a conceit their drink tastes better
In an outlandish cup than in our own,   55
So methinks every kiss she gives me now
In this strange form, is worth a pair of two.
Here we are safe, and furthest from the eye
Of all suspicion, this is my father's chamber,
Upon which floor he never steps till night: 60
Here he mistrusts me not, nor I his coming;
At mine own chamber he still pries unto me;
My freedom is not there at mine own finding,
Still checked and curbed; here he shall miss his purpose.

MOLL

And what's your business, now you have your mind, sir?   65
At your great suit I promised you to come,
I pitied her for name's sake, that a Moll
Should be so crossed in love when there's so many

47 *to choose* for choice
59 *father's* ed. (fathets Q)
62 *still* always
65 *business, now* ed. (business now, Q)

---

49 *Many an old madam.* Doublets were occasionally worn by women (without the pretence of being dressed as men), but whether especially by bawds seems unrecorded.

57 *pair of two.* This has sometimes been amended to 'pair or two'; but 'pair' could mean a set of indeterminate number, and I have occasionally heard 'pair of two' in colloquial speech quite recently. The amendment somewhat weakens Sebastian's gesture.

That owes nine lays apiece, and not so little:
My tailor fitted her, how like you his work?   70

SEBASTIAN

So well, no art can mend it for this purpose;
But to thy wit and help we're chief in debt,
And must live still beholding.

MOLL   Any honest pity
I'm willing to bestow upon poor ring-doves.

SEBASTIAN

I'll offer no worse play.

MOLL   Nay, and you should, sir,   75
I should draw first and prove the quicker man.

SEBASTIAN

Hold, there shall need no weapon at this meeting,
But 'cause thou shalt not loose thy fury idle,
Here take this viol, run upon the guts,
And end thy quarrel singing.

MOLL   Like a swan above bridge,   80
For look you here's the bridge, and here am I.

SEBASTIAN

Hold on, sweet Moll.

MARY

I've heard her much commended, sir, for one that was ne'er
taught.

MOLL

I'm much beholding to 'em: well since you'll needs put us   85
together, sir, I'll play my part as well as I can: it shall ne'er
be said I came into a gentleman's chamber and let his instrument hang by the walls.

SEBASTIAN

Why well said, Moll, i'faith, it had been a shame for that
gentleman then, that would have let it hung still and   90
ne'er offered thee it.

MOLL

There it should have been still then for Moll, for though the
world judge impudently of me, I ne'er came into that

---

69 *lays*. Bullen glosses 'wagers', but a sexual meaning seems more likely.
78 *'cause thou shalt not loose thy fury idle*. There is probably a play here on
   'fury' in the sense of (musical) inspiration. cf. Morley, *Introduction to
   Music* (1597), 35: 'This hath been a mighty musical fury, which hath
   caused him to show such diversity in so small bounds'. Thus, 'so that
   your passion is not wasted'.
80 *a swan above bridge*. Swans were plentiful in the London reaches of the
   Thames.

chamber yet where I took down the instrument myself.
SEBASTIAN
    Pish, let 'em prate abroad, th'art here where thou art known   95
    and loved: there be a thousand close dames that will call the
    viol an unmannerly instrument for a woman, and therefore
    talk broadly of thee, when you shall have them sit wider to a
    worse quality.
MOLL
    Push, I ever fall asleep and think not of 'em, sir, and thus I   100
    dream.
SEBASTIAN
Prithee let's hear thy dream, Moll.
MOLL

    I dream there is a mistress,   *The song*
      And she lays out the money,
    She goes unto her sisters,   105
      She never comes at any.

      Enter SIR ALEXANDER *behind them*

    She says she went to the Burse for patterns,
    You shall find her at Saint Kathern's,
      And comes home with never a penny.
SEBASTIAN
That's a free mistress, faith.   110
SIR ALEXANDER
    [*Aside*] Ay, ay, ay, like her that sings it, one of thine own
    choosing.

  98 *when you shall have them sit wider*. The instrument is a gamba, played at
     this period with the body of the viol gripped between the player's thighs
     or knees (cf. *A Trick to Catch the Old One*, I.i, 133); the sexual punning
     on 'instrument' reaches its home in this line.
 107 *the Burse*. Bullen suggests the Earl of Salisbury's New Exchange in the
     Strand (built 1609), above which were drapery and haberdashery
     shops; but the date makes it much more likely that the allusion is to the
     Royal Exchange, built (on the site in Cornhill) by Sir Thomas Gresham
     in 1567, and this is confirmed by a reference in *A Chaste Maid*, I.ii, 34:
     'As if she lay with all the gaudy shops/In Gresham's Burse about her'.
 108 *Saint Kathern's*. Perhaps an allusion to St Katherine's Fair, which,
     until the late sixteenth century, had been held to provide funds for St
     Katherine's Hospital on Tower Hill. The hospital precinct had a
     prison called St Katherine's Hole. The whole area had by the seventeenth
     century a generally bad reputation. In *The Alchemist* (V.iii, 55f.) St
     Kathern's is said to be 'where they use to keep/The better sort of mad
     folks'.

MOLL

But shall I dream again?
>Here comes a wench will brave ye,
>>Her courage was so great,   115
>She lay with one o' the navy,
>>Her husband lying i'the Fleet.
>Yet oft with him she cavilled,
>>I wonder what she ails,
>Her husband's ship lay gravelled,   120
>>When hers could hoise up sails,
>Yet she began like all my foes
>To call whore first: for so do those,
>>A pox of all false tails.

SEBASTIAN

Marry, amen say I.   125

SIR ALEXANDER

So say I too.

MOLL

Hang up the viol now, sir: all this while I was in a dream, one
shall lie rudely then; but being awake, I keep my legs
together. A watch, what's o'clock here?

SIR ALEXANDER

Now, now she's trapped.   130

MOLL

Between one and two: nay then I care not: a watch and a
musician are cousin-germans in one thing, they must both
keep time well, or there's no goodness in 'em; the one else
deserves to be dashed against a wall, and t'other to have his
brains knocked out with a fiddle case. What, a loose chain   135
and a dangling diamond? Here were a brave booty for an
evening-thief now, there's many a younger brother would be
glad to look twice in at a window for't, and wriggle in and
out like an eel in a sandbag. Oh, if men's secret youthful
faults should judge 'em, 'twould be the general'st execution   140

---

117 *i'the Fleet* i.e., in the prison
124 *tails* cant term for sexual organs and so extended to their owners;
      here with a play on 'tales'
132 *cousin-germans* first cousins
136 ff. prose ed. (arranged as rough verse Q)

---

139 *like an eel in a sandbag*. A proverbial phrase used of things languishing
   for want of proper sustenance. cf. Jonson, *Cynthia's Revels*, II.v, 18ff.:
   'all the ladies and gallants lie languishing upon the rushes ... and
   without we return quickly, they are all, as a youth would say, no better
   than a few trouts cast ashore, or a dish of eels in a sandbag'.

that ere was seen in England; there would be but few left to
sing the ballets, there would be so much work: most of our
brokers would be chosen for hangmen, a good day for them:
they might renew their wardropes of free cost then.

SEBASTIAN
This is the roaring wench must do us good.   145

MARY
No poison, sir, but serves us for some use,
Which is confirmed in her.

SEBASTIAN   Peace, peace.
Foot, I did hear him sure, where'er he be.

MOLL
Who did you hear?

SEBASTIAN   My father.
'Twas like a sight of his, I must be wary.   150

SIR ALEXANDER
No, wilt not be. Am I alone so wretched
That nothing takes? I'll put him to his plunge for't.

SEBASTIAN
Life, here he comes.—Sir, I beseech you take it,
Your way of teaching does so much content me,
I'll make it four pound, here's forty shillings, sir: 155
I think I name it right (help me, good Moll),
Forty in hand.

MOLL   Sir, you shall pardon me,
I have more of the meanest scholar I can teach,
This pays me more than you have offered yet.

SEBASTIAN
At the next quarter   160
When I receive the means my father 'lows me,
You shall have t'other forty.

SIR ALEXANDER   This were well now,
Were't to a man whose sorrows had blind eyes,
But mine behold his follies and untruths

142 *ballets* ballads
143 *brokers* pawnbrokers or jobbers, but also pimps
148 *Foot* i.e., 's foot (for 'God's foot')
150 *sight* sigh
152 *to his plunge* into a dilemma
159 *This* sc. the meanest scholar

144 *wardropes.* A variant form of 'wardrobe'; but *OED* gives independently
   'a rope for some mechanical purpose', and the intended quibble is evident.
162–3 cf. *The Honest Whore*, part 1, II.i, 277: 'This were well now, to one
   but newly fledged'.

With two clear glasses.—How now?   [*Comes forward*]
SEBASTIAN   Sir.   165
SIR ALEXANDER   What's he there?
SEBASTIAN

You're come in good time, sir, I've a suit to you,
I'd crave your present kindness.
SIR ALEXANDER   What is he there?
SEBASTIAN

A gentleman, a musician, sir, one of excellent fingering.
SIR ALEXANDER

[*Aside*] Ay, I think so, I wonder how they scaped her.
SEBASTIAN

Has the most delicate stroke, sir.   170
SIR ALEXANDER

A stroke indeed, I feel it at my heart.
SEBASTIAN

Puts down all your famous musicians.
SIR ALEXANDER

Ay, a whore may put down a hundred of 'em.
SEBASTIAN

Forty shillings is the agreement, sir, between us:
Now sir, my present means mounts but to half on't.   175
SIR ALEXANDER

And he stands upon the whole.
SEBASTIAN   Ay indeed does he, sir.
SIR ALEXANDER

And will do still, he'll ne'er be in other tale.
SEBASTIAN

Therefore I'd stop his mouth, sir, and I could.
SIR ALEXANDER

Hum, true, there is no other way indeed;—
[*Aside*] His folly hardens, shame must needs succeed.   180
—Now sir, I understand you profess music.

169 *how they scaped her* i.e., how she, supposed light-fingered, man-
    aged not to pick up the jewels, etc., laid out to trap her
172 *Puts down* (1) surpasses, (2) overthrows, with a hint of the sexual
    disease she may give them
177 *And will . . . tale* i.e., he'll not be paid: he will always be in that
    position, there will be no other reckoning
178 *and* chiefly in the sense of 'if', but a play on the other sense is
    pleasant

174 *Forty shillings is the agreement.* This seems not to square with the trick
    thought up earlier (ll.155ff.)

MOLL

I am a poor servant to that liberal science, sir.

SIR ALEXANDER

Where is it you teach?

MOLL   Right against Clifford's Inn.

SIR ALEXANDER

Hum, that's a fit place for it: you have many scholars?

MOLL

And some of worth, whom I may call my masters.   185

SIR ALEXANDER

[*Aside*] Ay true, a company of whoremasters.

—You teach to sing too?

MOLL   Marry do I sir.

SIR ALEXANDER

I think you'll find an apt scholar of my son, especially for
prick-song.

MOLL

I have much hope of him.   190

SIR ALEXANDER

[*Aside*] I am sorry for't, I have the less for that.—You can
play any lesson?

MOLL

At first sight, sir.

SIR ALEXANDER

There's a thing called the witch, can you play that?

MOLL

I would be sorry anyone should mend me in't.   195

SIR ALEXANDER

[*Aside*] Ay, I believe thee, thou hast so bewitched my son,

192 *lesson* a musical exercise or composition specially written for
    teaching
194 *the witch* this seems to have been the name of several popular
    pieces
195 *mend* probably in the sense of 'surpass', though 'improve' is possible

---

183 *Clifford's Inn*, next to the church of St Dunstan in the West, Fleet Street,
    was the oldest inn in Chancery: it was the seat of all six attorneys of the
    Palace Court, and it was said that more misery emanated from this
    small spot than from any one of the most populous counties in England
    (*Old and New London*, I, 92).
187 *You teach to sing too.* i.e., in the low sense, to copulate (see *Sh. Bawdy*,
    187). cf. *A Chaste Maid*, II.i, 52, and *Troilus and Cressida*, V.ii, 9ff.
189 *prick-song.* Music sung from notes written or 'pricked', as distinguished
    from that learnt by ear. Sexual quibbles on this word are legion in con-
    temporary plays.

No care will mend the work that thou hast done:
I have bethought myself, since my art fails,
I'll make her policy the art to trap her.
Here are four angels marked with holes in them   200
Fit for his cracked companions, gold he will give her,
These will I make induction to her ruin,
And rid shame from my house, grief from my heart.
—Here son, in what you take content and pleasure,
Want shall not curb you; pay the gentleman   205
His latter half in gold.
SEBASTIAN   I thank you, sir.
SIR ALEXANDER
[*Aside*] Oh may the operation on't end three:
In her, life; shame in him; and grief in me.
                                        Exit [SIR] ALEXANDER
SEBASTIAN
Faith thou shalt have 'em, 'tis my father's gift,
Never was man beguiled with better shift.   210
MOLL
He that can take me for a male musician,
I cannot choose but make him my instrument
And play upon him.   *Exeunt omnes*

[Act IV, Scene ii]

Enter MISTRESS GALLIPOT, *and* MISTRESS OPENWORK

MISTRESS GALLIPOT
Is then that bird of yours, Master Goshawk, so wild?
MISTRESS OPENWORK
A goshawk, a puttock, all for prey; he angles for fish, but he
loves flesh better.

---

200 *angels marked with holes in them.* The holes are evidently punched
    through the middle (see V.ii, 240). The trick seems to be to land Moll
    either with spoiled coins, the possession of which would be an offence,
    or with marked ones which could later be sworn to be stolen. Angels
    were at this time worth 10 shillings.
212–13 *make him my instrument And play upon him.* Another reminiscence of
    Hamlet (cf. III.ii, 366).
  2 *puttock.* Kite or buzzard, but applied generally to birds of prey. Gos-
    hawks (which were once commoner in England than now) are not fish-
    eaters, but could well have been confused with ospreys or even, by
    such as Mistress Openwork, with herons. 'Fish' has long been cant for
    loose women or female genitals.

MISTRESS GALLIPOT
Is't possible his smooth face should have wrinkles in't, and
we not see them?   5
MISTRESS OPENWORK
Possible? why, have not many handsome legs in silk stockings
villainous splay feet for all their great roses?
MISTRESS GALLIPOT
Troth sirrah, thou sayst true.
MISTRESS OPENWORK
Didst never see an archer, as thou'st walked by Bunhill, look
a-squint when he drew his bow?   10
MISTRESS GALLIPOT
Yes, when his arrows have fline toward Islington, his eyes
have shot clean contrary towards Pimlico.
MISTRESS OPENWORK
For all the world, so does Master Goshawk double with me.
MISTRESS GALLIPOT
Oh fie upon him, if he double once he's not for me.

7 *roses* knots of ribbons worn on the shoe (still, or again, fashionable
   in Jane Austen's time): see the illustration on the title-page
9 *thou'st* ed. (tho'ast Q)
11 *fline* flown
13 *double* use duplicity, act deceitfully

---

4 *his smooth face.* cf. Dekker's *Seven Deadly Sins of London* (1606), V, 36:
   'They knew how smooth soever his looks were, there was a devil in his
   bosom'.
6 *silk stockings.* Stubbes and other puritans were particularly severe on the
   extravagance of silk stockings 'curiously knit with open seam down the
   leg, with quirks and clocks about the ankles, and sometime (haply)
   interlaced with gold or silver threads . . . The time hath been, when one
   might have clothed all his body well, from top to toe, for less than a
   pair of these nether stocks will cost' (*Anatomy of Abuses*, 31).
9 *Bunhill.* The old artillery ground, next to the famous cemetery, just
   west of the site of Finsbury Square, was regularly used for archery
   matches. Bullen quotes from the *Remembrancia* that, in September
   1623, Middleton received 20 marks 'for his services at the shooting on
   Bunhill, and at the Conduit Head before the Lord Mayor and Aldermen'.
12 *Pimlico.* Not the familiar one near Victoria, but a part of Hoxton
   between New North Road and Hoxton Street. It was much frequented
   'for the sake of the fresh air and the cakes and ale for which it was
   famous' (Sugden). cf. Jonson, *The Alchemist*, V.ii, 17ff.: 'Gallants, men,
   and women,/And of all sorts, tag-rag, been seen to flock here/In threaves,
   these ten weeks, as to a second Hogsden, In days of Pimlico'. There are
   many contemporary references. The name may originally have been
   that of the owner of an alehouse.

MISTRESS OPENWORK

Because Goshawk goes in a shag-ruff band, with a face   15
sticking up in't which shows like an agate set in a cramp-
ring, he thinks I'm in love with him.

MISTRESS GALLIPOT

'Las, I think he takes his mark amiss in thee.

MISTRESS OPENWORK

He has by often beating into me made me believe that my
husband kept a whore.   20

MISTRESS GALLIPOT

Very good.

MISTRESS OPENWORK

Swore to me that my husband this very morning went in a
boat with a tilt over it, to the Three Pigeons at Brainford, and
his punk with him under his tilt.

MISTRESS GALLIPOT

That were wholesome.   25

MISTRESS OPENWORK

I believed it, fell a-swearing at him, cursing of harlots, made
me ready to hoise up sail and be there as soon as he.

MISTRESS GALLIPOT

So, so.

MISTRESS OPENWORK

And for that voyage Goshawk comes hither incontinently:
but sirrah, this water-spaniel dives after no duck but me, his   30
hope is having me at Brainford to make me cry quack.

MISTRESS GALLIPOT

Art sure of it?

MISTRESS OPENWORK

Sure of it? my poor innocent Openwork came in as I was
poking my ruff, presently hit I him i'the teeth with the Three
Pigeons: he forswore all, I up and opened all, and now stands   35

23 *tilt* an awning over a boat
29 *incontinently* straightway, punning on the sense of unable to resist
    sexual appetite
34 *poking my ruff* crimping the folds of the ruff with a poking-stick, a
    rod made of horn, bone, or latterly of steel so that it could be
    applied hot

16–17 *an agate set in a cramp-ring.* Cramp-rings were worn on the finger as
    a protection against cramp and falling-sickness: in pre-Reformation
    times they were hallowed each Good Friday by the king or queen. For
    the slang use, see V.i, 204.

he in a shop hard by, like a musket on a rest, to hit Goshawk
i'the eye, when he comes to fetch me to the boat.

MISTRESS GALLIPOT

Such another lame gelding offered to carry me through
thick and thin—Laxton, sirrah—but I am rid of him now.

MISTRESS OPENWORK

Happy is the woman can be rid of 'em all; 'las, what are your   40
whisking gallants to our husbands, weigh 'em rightly man for
man?

MISTRESS GALLIPOT

Troth, mere shallow things.

MISTRESS OPENWORK

Idle simple things, running heads, and yet let 'em run over us
never so fast, we shopkeepers, when all's done, are sure to   45
have 'em in our purse-nets at length, and when they are in,
Lord, what simple animals they are.

[MISTRESS GALLIPOT   ]

---

41 *whisking* smart or lively
44 *running* flighty, perhaps with a secondary sense of fluent or plausible

---

36 *like a musket on a rest.* The old matchlock musket was very heavy and
needed a rest to support the barrel to ensure accuracy of aim; it con-
sisted of a wooden pole with an iron fork at the upper end to rest the
musket in, and a spike at the bottom to fix it in the ground. The soldier
carried it by a lanyard over his shoulder.

46 *purse-nets.* Bag-shaped nets of which the mouth could be drawn together
with a string: they were used especially for catching rabbits. 'Rabbit' or
'coney' was also thieves' cant for a dupe and the purse-net a device by
which he was caught (see Greene's *Notable Discovery of Cozenage* (1591)
in Judges, at p. 136). cf. also *The Gull's Horn-Book*, I: 'a rich man's
son shall no sooner be out of the shell of his minority but he shall
straightways be . . . ta'en in his own purse-nets by fencers and coney-
catchers'.

48ff. Something is at fault in Q here, for Mistress Openwork is given two
consecutive speeches. The second, 'Then they hang the head', is at the
top of a page, and the catchword on the previous page is, accordingly,
the speech heading. I agree with Price (Manuscript and Quarto) in
thinking that some short speech by Mistress Gallipot—which might
give the dialogue a more obvious sequence at this point—has accidentally been omitted, though at what stage cannot be ascertained. Three
copies of Q have been reset at this point (see Bowers, 106–7) and read,
among other accidentals, 'Then they hang head' (l. 49) and 'Then they
deal' (l.53). Perhaps someone spotted the inconsequence of the un-
corrected text, found after all that it couldn't be easily corrected, but in
unlocking the forme allowed the type to loosen and pie, and reset it
carelessly: the 'corrected' phrases have no authority.

MISTRESS OPENWORK
Then they hang the head.

MISTRESS GALLIPOT
Then they droop.   50

MISTRESS OPENWORK
Then they write letters.

MISTRESS GALLIPOT
Then they cog.

MISTRESS OPENWORK
Then deal they underhand with us, and we must ingle with
our husbands abed, and we must swear they are our cousins,
and able to do us a pleasure at court.   55

MISTRESS GALLIPOT
And yet when we have done our best, all's but put into a
riven dish, we are but frumped at and libelled upon.

MISTRESS OPENWORK
Oh if it were the good Lord's will, there were a law made no
citizen should trust any of 'em at all.

Enter GOSHAWK

MISTRESS GALLIPOT
Hush sirrah, Goshawk flutters.   60

GOSHAWK
How now, are you ready?

MISTRESS OPENWORK
Nay are you ready? a little thing you see makes us ready.

GOSHAWK
Us? why, must she make one i'the voyage?

MISTRESS OPENWORK
Oh by any means: do I know how my husband will handle
me?   65

GOSHAWK
[*Aside*] Foot, how shall I find water to keep these two mills
going?—Well, since you'll needs be clapped under hatches, if

52 *cog* fawn, wheedle
53 *ingle* coax, cajole
57 *riven* split (the dish of the image would be a wooden trencher)
57 *frumped at* mocked, insulted, browbeaten
67 *clapped under hatches* kept down or in silence; but 'clap' was used
    catachrestically for 'clip' (= embrace)

49 *Then they hang the head. Then they droop.* The sexual innuendoes in this
    passage are made plain here: even now the intentions of the two ladies
    cannot be taken at face value.

I sail not with you both till all split, hang me up at the main-
yard and duck me.—It's but liquoring them both soundly,
and then you shall see their cork heels fly up high, like two   70
swans when their tails are above water, and their long necks
under water, diving to catch gudgeons.—Come, come, oars
stand ready, the tide's with us, on with those false faces; blow
winds and thou shalt take thy husband casting out his net to
catch fresh salmon at Brainford.   75

MISTRESS GALLIPOT

I believe you'll eat of a cod's head of your own dressing
before you reach half way thither.   [*They mask themselves*]

GOSHAWK

So, so, follow close, pin as you go.

Enter LAXTON *muffled*

LAXTON

Do you hear?

MISTRESS GALLIPOT

Yes, I thank my ears.   80

LAXTON

I must have a bout with your pothecaryship.

MISTRESS GALLIPOT

At what weapon?

LAXTON

I must speak with you.

MISTRESS GALLIPOT

No.

LAXTON

No? you shall.   85

MISTRESS GALLIPOT

Shall? away, soused sturgeon, half fish, half flesh.

72 *gudgeons* doubtless with a play on the sense of (easily caught)
   simpletons (cf. *A Chaste Maid in Cheapside*, IV.ii, 53)
73 *false faces* masks

---

68 *till all split.* Till all suffer shipwreck, or go to pieces: originally, as here,
   a sailors' phrase, though soon made over into common use. cf. *A Mid-
   summer Night's Dream*, I.ii, 32, and *A Chaste Maid*, IV.ii, 95.
70 *cork heels.* Chopines had cork soles and high cork heels; they were worn
   outdoors as a fashionable alternative to clogs.
76 *you'll eat of a cod's head of your own dressing.* You'll make a fool of yourself, caught in your own net: a cod's head is a stupid fellow, but Mistress
   Gallipot must want him to be tricked into picking up the sexual suggestion.
81 *bout* would normally imply a sexual encounter, but we know this is not
   Laxton's way with Mistress Gallipot.

LAXTON
>   'Faith, gib, are you spitting? I'll cut your tail, puss-cat, for
>   this.

MISTRESS GALLIPOT
>   'Las poor Laxton, I think thy tail's cut already: you're
>   worsed.   90

LAXTON
>   If I do not—   *Exit* LAXTON

GOSHAWK
>   Come, ha' you done?

Enter MASTER OPENWORK

>   'Sfoot Rosamond, your husband.

MASTER OPENWORK
>   How now? sweet Master Goshawk, none more welcome,
>   I have wanted your embracements: when friends meet,
>   The music of the spheres sounds not more sweet   95
>   Than does their conference; who is this? Rosamond?
>   Wife? how now, sister?

GOSHAWK   Silence if you love me.

MASTER OPENWORK
>   Why masked?

MISTRESS OPENWORK   Does a mask grieve you, sir?

MASTER OPENWORK   It does.

MISTRESS OPENWORK
>   Then y'are best get you a-mumming.

GOSHAWK   'Sfoot, you'll spoil all.

MISTRESS GALLIPOT
>   May not we cover our bare faces with masks   100
>   As well as you cover your bald heads with hats?

MASTER OPENWORK
>   No: masks, why, th'are thieves to beauty, that rob eyes

---

87 *gib* cat, hence a term of reproach for a scold
94 *wanted your embracements* missed your company
102 *No: masks,* ed. (No masks, Q)

89–90 *you're worsed* ed. (your worst Q). You're blemished or worsed. The
     Q reading could be understood as an abbreviated challenge—'do your
     worst'—but 'worst' is a regular form of the past participle of the old
     verb 'to worse', and this seems to fit best with the remainder of the line.
99 *get you a-mumming.* The phrase 'to go a-mumming' means to disguise
     oneself, especially for a mumming play, which was acted with masks in
     dumb-show: perhaps, therefore, 'you'd best keep silence'. (To play or
     keep mum meant, as now, to be silent.)

Of admiration in which true love lies.
Why are masks worn, why good, or why desired,
Unless by their gay covers wits are fired   105
To read the vildest looks? Many bad faces
(Because rich gems are treasured up in cases)
Pass by their privilege current: but as caves
Dam misers' gold, so masks are beauty's graves;
Men ne'er meet women with such muffled eyes,   110
But they curse her that first did masks devise,
And swear it was some beldam. Come, off with't.

MISTRESS OPENWORK
I will not.

MASTER OPENWORK
Good faces masked are jewels kept by sprites:
Hide none but bad ones, for they poison men's sights,   115

---

112 *beldam* witch
114 *sprites* ed. (spirits Q), sc. evil spirits

104–6 Punctuation ed. (Why are maskes worne? why good? or why desired?
          Vnlesse by their gay couers wits are fiered
          To read the vild'st looks; Q)
The parallelism strongly suggests that here, as often elsewhere, Q has
anticipated the end of the question, though the proposed reading is
admittedly obscure in detail. I take it that Openwork's question means
'Why are masks worn unless wits are fired by them to take the gay outer
cover as earnest of the inner (which may be vile)?' If the Q punctuation
is retained, however, line 105 would go with what follows, and we
should then understand 'Unless wits are inspired to read through gay
covers (masks) and spot that there will be vile looks beneath, many bad
faces will get by because it will be assumed that, like jewels kept in
cases, something rich is concealed by the mask'. An attractive possibility is that for 'looks' in l. 106 we should read 'books': 'masks would
be desired because they would catch men, as a gay cover might trap
wits into reading trash'. But in the seventeenth century books had
covers which could hardly be called gay.

108 *Pass by their privilege current.* i.e., are received as genuine or honest,
because of the privilege conferred by masks. Masks were widely used by
prostitutes to spread their business, but they did not always enable
them to pass current: see *Northward Ho!*, I.ii, 83: 'we [whores] are not
current till we pass from one man to another'; and *The Honest Whore*,
part 2, IV.i, 397f.: 'She (crowned with reverend praises) passed by
them, I (though with face masked) could not scape the hem'.

109 *Dam.* The Q reading is 'dambe', which *OED* records only as an erron-
eous form of 'dam', though 'damb' is found for 'damn'. Doubtless
there is a *double entendre*, but the primary sense seems best served by
'dam': misers' gold is blocked up, obscured, in caves.

Show them as shopkeepers do their broidered stuff,
By owl-light; fine wares cannot be open enough:
Prithee, sweet Rose, come strike this sail.

MISTRESS OPENWORK   Sail?

MASTER OPENWORK   Ha!
Yes wife, strike sail, for storms are in thine eyes.

MISTRESS OPENWORK
Th'are here, sir, in my brows if any rise.   120

MASTER OPENWORK
Ha, brows? what says she, friend? pray tell me why
Your two flags were advanced; the comedy,
Come, what's the comedy?

MISTRESS GALLIPOT   *Westward Ho.*

MASTER OPENWORK   How?

MISTRESS OPENWORK
'Tis *Westward Ho* she says.

GOSHAWK   Are you both mad?

MISTRESS OPENWORK
Is't market day at Brainford, and your ware   125
Not sent up yet?

MASTER OPENWORK What market day? what ware?

MISTRESS OPENWORK
A pie with three pigeons in't, 'tis drawn and stays your
cutting up.

GOSHAWK
As you regard my credit—

MASTER OPENWORK
Art mad?   130

MISTRESS OPENWORK
Yes, lecherous goat, baboon.

---

116 *them* ed. (then Q): bad faces ought only to be shown by **owl-light**
when, like the inferior quality of shopkeepers' embroidery, they
can't be clearly seen

120 *in my brows* perhaps a remote allusion to a female cuckold's (or
cuckquean's) horns   123 s.p. MISTRESS GALLIPOT ed. (Mist. Open. Q)

127 *stays your cutting up* cf. III.ii, 228 and n.

131 *baboon* a generalized term of abuse

---

122 *Your two flags*. Flags with individual symbols were hoisted on the tops
of theatres an hour or two before a play was due to begin; there is
presumably also a play on the flag that a boat might carry, and possibly
on the slang meaning of apron.

123 *Westward Ho*. By Dekker and Webster (1604–05). 'Westward ho!' was
the cry of watermen going west, as for example towards Brentford from
London. cf. *Twelfth Night*, III.i, 146.

MASTER OPENWORK
Baboon? then toss me in a blanket.
MISTRESS OPENWORK
Do I it well?
MISTRESS GALLIPOT
Rarely.
GOSHAWK
Belike, sir, she's not well; best leave her.
MASTER OPENWORK   No,   135
I'll stand the storm now how fierce so e'er it blow.
MISTRESS OPENWORK
Did I for this lose all my friends? refuse
Rich hopes and golden fortunes, to be made
A stale to a common whore?
MASTER OPENWORK   This does amaze me.
MISTRESS OPENWORK
Oh God, oh God, feed at reversion now?   140
A strumpet's leaving?
MASTER OPENWORK   Rosamond.
GOSHAWK
I sweat, would I lay in Cold Harbour.
MISTRESS OPENWORK
Thou hast struck ten thousand daggers through my heart.
MASTER OPENWORK
Not I, by heaven, sweet wife.
MISTRESS OPENWORK   Go, devil, go;
That which thou swear'st by damns thee.   145

---

140 *at reversion* (in legal terms) in succession, conditionally on the
     expiry of a grant or at death; but reversions are also the left-overs
     of a dish or meal

---

132 *toss me in a blanket.* Tossing in a blanket was a 'rough, irregular form of
     punishment' (*OED*), the offender being thrown repeatedly in the air
     from a blanket held slackly from the corners. There is probably a play
     on blanket-love, meaning illicit amours.
139 *stale.* A mistress turned to ridicule for the amusement of a rival; but the
     whole phrase telescopes this with the sense of 'common stale', a pros-
     titute used by thieves as a decoy.
142 *Cold Harbour.* The name of a former mansion in Upper Thames Street,
     which passed through the hands of a remarkable number of noble
     owners and was replaced in the mid-sixteenth century by a collection
     of tenements which quickly became a haunt of poverty and an ad-hoc
     sanctuary for those wanting to disappear, as undoubtedly Goshawk
     wants at this moment (the alternative spelling 'Cole' can mean a cheat);
     but he is of course playing on the literal meaning of the name.

GOSHAWK
  'S heart, will you undo me?
MISTRESS OPENWORK
  Why stay you here? the star by which you sail
  Shines yonder above Chelsea, you lose your shore;
  If this moon light you, seek out your light whore.
MASTER OPENWORK
  Ha?
MISTRESS OPENWORK   Push, your western pug—
GOSHAWK   Zounds, now hell roars. 150
MISTRESS OPENWORK
  With whom you tilted in a pair of oars,
  This very morning.
MASTER OPENWORK   Oars?
MISTRESS OPENWORK   At Brainford, sir.
MASTER OPENWORK
  Rack not my patience: Master Goshawk,
  Some slave has buzzed this into her, has he not?
  I run a tilt in Brainford with a woman?   155
  'Tis a lie:
  What old bawd tells thee this? 'Sdeath, 'tis a lie.
MISTRESS OPENWORK
  'Tis one to thy face shall justify all that I speak.
MASTER OPENWORK
  Ud'soul, do but name that rascal.
MISTRESS OPENWORK
  No sir, I will not.

150 s.p. MISTRESS OPENWORK ed. (Mist. Gal. Q)
150 *western pug* (png Q) a pug is a harlot, but Western pugs were
    bargees who navigated barges down the Thames to London, as
    from Brentford among other places
151 *tilted* jousted, but also (of a boat) pitched in the waves; and cf.
    above 1.23, and *1 Henry IV*, II.iii, 93, 'to tilt with lips'
155 *run a tilt* (or run a-tilt) engage in a tilt or joust
159 *Ud'soul* God's soul

147ff. For thirty lines (147–78) Q prints a medley of verse and prose: the
    rhymes, some evident pentameters, an occasional median capital, and
    the fact that some is printed as verse suggest that it should all be,
    though the result is undoubtedly rough.
147–9 *the star . . . whore.* Punctuation ed. (star, . . . sail, . . . Chelsea; . . .
    light you: . . . whore. Q) I take it that this means 'you are missing your
    landing by not attending to the star in the west; if that's the way you
    want to go, now is the time'.
158 *'Tis one to thy face* (stet Q). Bullen suggests ' 'Tis one who to thy
    face . . .'

GOSHAWK   Keep thee there, girl:—then!   160
MASTER OPENWORK
  Sister, know you this varlet?
MISTRESS GALLIPOT   Yes.
MASTER OPENWORK   Swear true.
  Is there a rogue so low damned? a second Judas?
  A common hangman? cutting a man's throat?
  Does it to his face? bite me behind my back?
  A cur dog? swear if you know this hell-hound.   165
MISTRESS GALLIPOT
  In truth I do.
MASTER OPENWORK
                  His name?
MISTRESS GALLIPOT   Not for the world,
  To have you to stab him.
GOSHAWK   Oh brave girls, worth gold.
MASTER OPENWORK
  A word, honest Master Goshawk.   *Draw out his sword*
GOSHAWK   What do you mean, sir?
MASTER OPENWORK
  Keep off, and if the devil can give a name
  To this new fury, holla it through my ear,   170
  Or wrap it up in some hid character:
  I'll ride to Oxford and watch out mine eyes
  But I'll hear the brazen head speak: or else
  Show me but one hair of his head or beard,
  That I may sample it; if the fiend I meet   175
  In mine own house, I'll kill him:—in the street,
  Or at the church door:—there ('cause he seeks to untie
  The knot God fastens) he deserves most to die.
MISTRESS OPENWORK
  My husband titles him.

161 s.p. MASTER OPENWORK ed. (Mis. Open. Q)
176 *in the street* ed. (the street Q)

---

167 *worth gold.* Proverbial: cf. Munday, *Fedele and Fortunio* (1585), l. 1703:
    'such a girl is worth gold in a dear year'; and the subtitle of Heywood's
    Fair Maid of the West—'A girl worth gold'.
172–3 *I'll ride to Oxford* ... Friar Bacon and Friar Bungay spent seven
    years making a brass head, so that they could ask it whether it were
    possible to build a wall of brass round Britain. Unfortunately they
    neglected to note the time at which the head was to speak and so received
    no distinct answer. cf. *The Famous Historie of Fryer Bacon* and Greene's
    Honourable History of Friar Bacon and Friar Bungay (to which Middle-
    ton had in 1602 written a prologue and epilogue), esp. sc. xi.

MASTER OPENWORK   Master Goshawk, pray sir,
  Swear to me that you know him or know him not,   180
  Who makes me at Brainford to take up a petticoat
  Besides my wife's.
GOSHAWK   By heaven that man I know not.
MISTRESS OPENWORK
  Come, come, you lie.
GOSHAWK   Will you not have all out?
  By heaven, I know no man beneath the moon
  Should do you wrong, but if I had his name,   185
  I'd print it in text letters.
MISTRESS OPENWORK   Print thine own then,
  Didst not thou swear to me he kept his whore?
MISTRESS GALLIPOT
  And that in sinful Brainford they would commit
  That which our lips did water at, sir,—ha?
MISTRESS OPENWORK
  Thou spider, that hast woven thy cunning web   190
  In mine own house t'insnare me: hast not thou
  Sucked nourishment even underneath this roof,
  And turned it all to poison, spitting it
  On thy friend's face (my husband), he as 'twere sleeping?
  Only to leave him ugly to mine eyes,   195
  That they might glance on thee?
MISTRESS GALLIPOT   Speak, are these lies?
GOSHAWK
  Mine own shame me confounds.
MASTER OPENWORK   No more, he's stung;
  Who'd think that in one body there could dwell
  Deformity and beauty, heaven and hell?
  Goodness I see is but outside: we all set,   200
  In rings of gold, stones that be counterfeit:
  I thought you none.
GOSHAWK   Pardon me.
MASTER OPENWORK   Truth I do.
  This blemish grows in nature, not in you,

186 *text letters* large or capital letters in handwriting
189 *our lips did water at* cf. III.ii, 20
197 s.p. MASTER OPENWORK ed. (Mist. Open. Q)

---

193 *turned it all to poison.* Spiders were commonly supposed to be poisonous,
  though, according to one view, only if known to be there. cf. *The*
  Winter's Tale, II.i, 40, and *No Wit, No Help, like a Woman's*, II.i,
  392–3.
201 *counterfeit.* Q has the spelling 'counterfet', which gives a perfect rhyme.

For man's creation sticks even moles in scorn
On fairest cheeks: wife, nothing is perfect born.   205

MISTRESS OPENWORK
I thought you had been born perfect.

MASTER OPENWORK
What's this whole world but a gilt rotten pill?
For at the heart lies the old chore still.
I'll tell you, Master Goshawk, in your eye
I have seen wanton fire, and then to try   210
The soundness of my judgment, I told you
I kept a whore, made you believe 'twas true,
Only to feel how your pulse beat, but find
The world can hardly yield a perfect friend.
Come, come, a trick of youth, and 'tis forgiven.   215
This rub put by, our love shall run more even.

MISTRESS OPENWORK
You'll deal upon men's wives no more?

GOSHAWK   No: you teach me
A trick for that.

MISTRESS OPENWORK   Troth do not, they'll o'erreach thee.

MASTER OPENWORK
Make my house yours, sir, still.

GOSHAWK   No.

MASTER OPENWORK   I say you shall:
Seeing thus besieged it holds out, 'twill never fall.   220

Enter MASTER GALLIPOT, *and* GREENWIT *like a sumner,* LAXTON
muffled aloof off

204 *sticks* ed. (sticke Q)
208 *chore* i.e., core, alluding here to Adam's apple
209 *in* ed. (I in Q)
217 *deal upon* set to work on, but to deal with a woman also means to
    have sexual intercourse with her
220 s.d. *sumner* (sommer Q, *corr. to* somner) an official employed to
    summon persons to appear in court

---

216 *rub.* Impediment: the image in the rest of the line suggests the physical
    rubs or roughnesses in a bowling alley, by which the bowls were
    deflected from their true course. cf. III.ii, 171 and n.
218 *A trick for that.* Perhaps as in the proverbial phrase 'a trick worth two of
    that'. (But cf. *A Trick to Catch the Old One*, IV.iv, 208.)
220 s.d., 230 The corrections at this point in three copies of Q (*somner* for
    sommer and *Crastino* for *Crastina*) for some reason involved the whole-
    sale resetting of the lower half of one page, though no other significant
    alterations of text are involved.

OMNES
  How now?
MASTER GALLIPOT
  With me, sir?
GREENWIT
  You, sir. I have gone snaffling up and down by your door this
  hour to watch for you.
MISTRESS GALLIPOT
  What's the matter, husband?   225
GREENWIT
  I have caught a cold in my head, sir, by sitting up late in the
  Rose tavern, but I hope you understand my speech.
MASTER GALLIPOT
  So sir.
GREENWIT
  I cite you by the name of Hippocrates Gallipot, and you by
  the name of Prudence Gallipot, to appear upon Crastino, do   230
  you see, Crastino sancti Dunstani (this Easter term) in Bow
  Church.
MASTER GALLIPOT
  Where, sir? what says he?
GREENWIT
  Bow: Bow Church, to answer to a libel of precontract on the

231 *Crastino sancti Dunstani* on the morrow of St Dunstan (i.e., 19
    May)
234 *libel* in ecclesiastical law, the plaintiff's written declaration of
    charges in a cause

---

223 *snaffling. OED* gives 'saunter' virtually on the strength of this line
    alone. But, as the reference to his cold three lines later shows, the word is
    simply a variant form of 'snuffling'—and one which is well represented
    in *OED*.
227 *Rose.* A fairly common name for inns and taverns: one stood on Holborn
    Hill, from which coaches departed for Brentford; Greenwit's may
    rather have been that near Temple Bar, frequented by lawyers.
229 *Hippocrates.* The name of the great Greek physician would be a suitable,
    if grandiose, one for an apothecary.
231–2 *Bow Church.* The famous church on the south side of Cheapside near
    the corner of Bread Street was formerly the seat of the Court of Arches,
    which, according to one tradition, was (like the church—St Mary-le-
    Bow or St Mary de Arcubus) named after the arched buttresses or bows
    which have always held up the steeple. But it may have sat in the early
    medieval crypt, the massive arches of which alone survived the Great
    Fire and were incorporated into Wren's rebuilding. (The crypt survived
    the blitz of 1940–44 also.) To this court came all appeals in ecclesiastical
    matters within the province of Canterbury.

part and behalf of the said Prudence and another: y'are best,   235
sir, take a copy of the citation, 'tis but twelvepence.

OMNES
A citation?

MASTER GALLIPOT
You pocky-nosed rascal, what slave fees you to this?

LAXTON
Slave? I ha' nothing to do with you, do you hear, sir?

GOSHAWK
Laxton, is't not?—what fagary is this?   240

MASTER GALLIPOT
Trust me, I thought, sir, this storm long ago
Had been full laid, when (if you be remembered)
I paid you the last fifteen pound, besides
The thirty you had first; for then you swore—

LAXTON
Tush, tush sir, oaths;   245
Truth, yet I'm loath to vex you,—tell you what:
Make up the money I had an hundred pound,
And take your bellyful of her.

MASTER GALLIPOT   An hundred pound?

MISTRESS GALLIPOT
What, a hundred pound? he gets none: what, a hundred
pound?

MASTER GALLIPOT
Sweet Pru, be calm, the gentleman offers thus,   250
If I will make the moneys that are past
A hundred pound, he will discharge all courts,
And give his bond never to vex us more.

MISTRESS GALLIPOT
A hundred pound? 'Las, take, sir, but threescore,
Do you seek my undoing?

LAXTON   I'll not bate one sixpence,—   255
I'll maul you, puss, for spitting.

MISTRESS GALLIPOT   Do thy worst,—
Will fourscore stop thy mouth?

LAXTON   No.

MISTRESS GALLIPOT   Y'are a slave,
Thou cheat, I'll now tear money from thy throat:
Husband, lay hold on yonder tawny-coat.

240 *fagary* i.e., vagary

---

259 *tawny-coat*. Ecclesiastical apparitors (servants of the court) wore tawny-
coloured livery.

GREENWIT

Nay, gentlemen, seeing your women are so hot, I must lose   260
my hair in their company, I see.   [*Takes off his wig*]

MISTRESS OPENWORK

His hair sheds off, and yet he speaks not so much in the nose
as he did before.

GOSHAWK

He has had the better chirurgeon.—Master Greenwit, is your
wit so raw as to play no better a part than a sumner's?   265

MASTER GALLIPOT

I pray, who plays a knack to know an honest man in this
company?

MISTRESS GALLIPOT

Dear husband, pardon me, I did dissemble,
Told thee I was his precontracted wife,
When letters came from him for thirty pound,   270
I had no shift but that.

MASTER GALLIPOT   A very clean shift:
But able to make me lousy. On.

MISTRESS GALLIPOT   Husband, I plucked
(When he had tempted me to think well of him)
Gelt feathers from thy wings, to make him fly
More lofty.

MASTER GALLIPOT

A' the top of you, wife: on.   275

MISTRESS GALLIPOT

He having wasted them, comes now for more,
Using me as a ruffian doth his whore,

271f. lineation ed. (prose Q)

260–1 *lose my hair*. Alluding to the most frequent and obvious effect of
syphilis. Q has 'loose', and the two words were indeed often not clearly
distinguished: a light pun is possible.

262 *in the nose*. cf. above, ll. 223 and 226; another effect of syphilis was to
make the nose swollen and pustular.

265 *no better a part than a sumner's*. Greene in his *Notable Discovery of
Cozenage* gives instances of coney-catchers learning a smattering of law
and going dressed as sumners or apparitors.

266 *A Knack to Know an Honest Man* is the title of an early anonymous
comedy; and the phrase and its complement, 'a knack to know a
knave', were in common proverbial use.

274 *Gelt* ed. (Get Q) The word, though coming rather from *geld* (= money),
was used occasionally for gold; but, like Dyce, I am by no means confident that the right reading has been restored. There might be an
allusion to gelding, of which 'gelt' was a common participial form.
Steevens suggests leaving the word out altogether.

Whose sin keeps him in breath: by heaven I vow
Thy bed he never wronged more than he does now.

MASTER GALLIPOT

My bed? ha, ha, like enough, a shop-board will serve   280
To have a cuckold's coat cut out upon:
Of that we'll talk hereafter—y'are a villain.

LAXTON

Hear me but speak, sir, you shall find me none.

OMNES

Pray sir, be patient and hear him.

MASTER GALLIPOT

I am muzzled for biting, sir, use me how you will.   285

LAXTON

The first hour that your wife was in my eye,
Myself with other gentlemen sitting by
In your shop tasting smoke, and speech being used
That men who have fairest wives are most abused
And hardly scaped the horn, your wife maintained   290
That only such spots in city dames were stained
Justly but by men's slanders: for her own part,
She vowed that you had so much of her heart,
No man by all his wit, by any wile
Never so fine spun, should yourself beguile   295
Of what in her was yours.

MASTER GALLIPOT   Yet, Pru, 'tis well:
Play out your game at Irish, sir: who wins?

MISTRESS OPENWORK

The trial is when she comes to bearing.

LAXTON

I scorned one woman thus should brave all men,
And (which more vexed me) a she-citizen.   300
Therefore I laid siege to her, out she held,
Gave many a brave repulse, and me compelled

297 *Irish* a game resembling backgammon (fully described in Cotton's
     Compleat Gamester of 1674)

---

290 *scaped* (scapt Q). The past form is influenced by 'abused' in the prev-
     ious line.

290–2 *your wife maintained* . . . Perhaps this means that she maintained
     that such stains on city dames came in truth only by slanders (cf.
     III.i, 84ff.).

298 *when she comes to bearing.* To bear at backgammon is to remove a piece
     at the end of a game: cf. *Northward Ho!*, IV.i, 267: 'she'd win any
     game when she came to bearing'. There is, of course, a quibble on bear-
     ing a child.

With shame to sound retreat to my hot lust;
Then seeing all base desires raked up in dust,
And that to tempt her modest ears I swore   305
Ne'er to presume again, she said her eye
Would ever give me welcome honestly,
And (since I was a gentleman) if it run low,
She would my state relieve, not to o'erthrow
Your own and hers: did so; then seeing I wrought   310
Upon her meekness, me she set at nought;
And yet to try if I could turn that tide,
You see what stream I strove with, but, sir, I swear
By heaven, and by those hopes men lay up there,
I neither have nor had a base intent   315
To wrong your bed; what's done is merriment:
Your gold I pay back with this interest,
When I had most power to do't I wronged you least.

MASTER GALLIPOT
    If this no gullery be, sir—

OMNES   No, no, on my life.

MASTER GALLIPOT
    Then, sir, I am beholden—not to you, wife—   320
    But Master Laxton, to your want of doing ill,
    Which it seems you have not. Gentlemen,
    Tarry and dine here all.

MASTER OPENWORK   Brother, we have a jest
    As good as yours to furnish out a feast.

MASTER GALLIPOT
    We'll crown our table with it: wife, brag no more   325
    Of holding out: who most brags is most whore.

                                          Exeunt omnes

---

317 *this interest* sc. the substance of the following line

[Act V, Scene i]

Enter JACK DAPPER, MOLL, SIR BEAUTEOUS GANYMEDE, *and* SIR
THOMAS LONG

JACK DAPPER

But prithee Master Captain Jack, be plain and perspicuous
with me: was it your Meg of Westminster's courage that
rescued me from the Poultry puttocks indeed?

MOLL

The valour of my wit, I ensure you, sir, fetched you off
bravely, when you were i'the forlorn hope among those   5
desperates. Sir Beauteous Ganymede here and Sir Thomas
Long heard that cuckoo, my man Trapdoor, sing the note of
your ransom from captivity.

SIR BEAUTEOUS

Uds so, Moll, where's that Trapdoor?

MOLL

Hanged I think by this time; a justice in this town, that   10
speaks nothing but 'Make a mittimus, away with him to
Newgate', used that rogue like a firework to run upon a line
betwixt him and me.

OMNES

How, how?

---

1 *perspicuous* clear in statement
5 *the forlorn hope* (Dutch *verloren hoop*) was originally a picked
body of men detached to the front to lead an attack, and hence
any group of men in a desperate state
11 *mittimus* a warrant under the hand of a J.P. ordering the person
named to be kept in custody until delivered to a court of law

---

2 *Meg of Westminster.* The exploits of this Meg (a heroine of somewhat
the same stamp as the Roaring Girl) are told in *The Life and Pranks of
Long Meg of Westminster*, 1582. A play about her was acted in 1594–95,
and she appears in the anti-masque of Jonson's *The Fortunate Isles*.
3 *Poultry puttocks.* The two kites were presumably attached to the
Poultry counter, in which Dekker was once imprisoned.
9 *Uds so.* The phrase has no specific meaning: 'Ud' as a form of the name
of God was attached to many other words and syllables in seventeenth-
century oaths, as Udsbud, Udshash, Udzooks. Uds so is probably a
transformation, ultimately, of catso: cf. III.ii, 153.
12 *a firework to run upon a line.* The expression, as Bullen notes, is not
uncommon. Dyce quotes from *The Whore of Babylon* (III.i, 89f.):
'Let us behold these fireworks that must run/Upon short lines of life'.
The line is a train or fuse of gunpowder (see l. 15) which combusts
along its length from one end to the other.

MOLL
>Marry, to lay trains of villainy to blow up my life; I smelt   15
>the powder, spied what linstock gave fire to shoot against
>the poor captain of the galley-foist, and away slid I my man
>like a shovel-board shilling. He struts up and down the
>suburbs I think, and eats up whores, feeds upon a bawd's
>garbage.   20

SIR THOMAS
>Sirrah Jack Dapper.

JACK DAPPER
>What sayst, Tom Long?

SIR THOMAS
>Thou hadst a sweet-faced boy, hail-fellow with thee, to your
>little Gull: how is he spent?

JACK DAPPER
>Troth I whistled the poor little buzzard off o' my fist,   25
>because when he waited upon me at the ordinaries, the
>gallants hit me i'the teeth still, and said I looked like a
>painted alderman's tomb, and the boy at my elbow like a
>death's head.—Sirrah Jack, Moll.

MOLL
>What says my little Dapper?   30

---

16 *linstock* a staff, very like a musket rest, which held a gunner's
   match or lunt
17 *galley-foist* a state barge, especially that of the Lord Mayor of
   London
25 *whistle off* a technical term in falconry, meaning to dismiss by
   whistling (cf. *Othello*, III.iii, 262)
27 *hit me i'the teeth* reproached or mocked me (cf. to throw it in one's
   teeth): cf. *A Fair Quarrel*, II.ii, 109

---

18 *shovel-board shilling.* Shovel-board, or shuffleboard, a game resembling
   shove-halfpenny in which silver pieces were knocked along a very long
   highly polished table into compartments marked out at the end, was
   widely popular. The coins most commonly used were Edward VI
   shillings (see *Merry Wives of Windsor*, I.i, 160), specially polished so
   that they were proverbially slippery. cf. Jonson, *Every Man in His
   Humour* (English version), III.v, 16–17, 'They . . . made it run as
   smooth off the tongue as a shove-groat shilling'.
26 *at the ordinaries.* cf. *The Gull's Horn-Book*, v, 'How a young gallant
   should behave himself in an ordinary'.
28 *a painted alderman's tomb.* The Elizabethan and early Stuart period was
   the great time for half-acre tombs, which were showily painted. A death's
   head is a common accompaniment of the effigies. Aldermen are promi-
   nent in Stow's copious lists of such monuments.

SIR BEAUTEOUS

Come, come, walk and talk, walk and talk.

JACK DAPPER

Moll and I'll be i'the midst.

MOLL

These knights shall have squires' places, belike then: well
Dapper, what say you?

JACK DAPPER

Sirrah Captain Mad Mary, the gull my own father, Dapper   35
Sir Davy, laid these London boot-halers, the catchpolls, in
ambush to set upon me.

OMNES

Your father? away, Jack.

JACK DAPPER

By the tassels of this handkercher 'tis true, and what was his
warlike stratagem, think you? He thought because a wicker   40
cage tames a nightingale, a lousy prison could make an ass
of me.

OMNES

A nasty plot.

JACK DAPPER

Ay: as though a counter, which is a park in which all the
wild beasts of the city run head by head, could tame me.   45

Enter the LORD NOLAND

MOLL

Yonder comes my Lord Noland.

OMNES

Save you, my Lord.

---

36 *boot-halers* freebooters or highwaymen; Dekker uses the word
   several times
36 *catchpolls* cf. III.i, 38
44 *counter* cf. III.iii, 72

---

33 *These knights . . . places.* Squires, as the knights' armour-bearers, would
   take their positions outside those whom they served.
35-6 *Dapper Sir Davy* ((Dapper) Sir Dauy Q). Perhaps we should read
   'Sir Davy Dapper', but Jack may be making a joke on his father's name.
39 *handkercher.* The customary spoken form of the word, particularly in
   Midland and southern dialect, until the eighteenth century, but common
   also in literary use (cf. *All's Well that Ends Well*, V.iii, 322). They were
   often extravagantly fringed and tasselled.
40-1 The analogy between the caged bird and imprisoned man was a
   commonplace. cf. *A Trick to Catch the Old One*, IV.iii, 48f. and Jonson,
   'To the World', 29ff.

LORD NOLAND

Well met, gentlemen all, good Sir Beauteous Ganymede, Sir
Thomas Long. And how does Master Dapper?

JACK DAPPER

Thanks, my Lord.   50

MOLL

No tobacco, my Lord?

LORD NOLAND

No 'faith, Jack.

JACK DAPPER

My Lord Noland, will you go to Pimlico with us? we are
making a boon voyage to that nappy land of spice-cakes.

LORD NOLAND

Here's such a merry ging, I could find in my heart to sail to   55
the world's end with such company; come, gentlemen, let's
on.

JACK DAPPER

Here's most amorous weather, my Lord.

OMNES

Amorous weather?   *They walk*

JACK DAPPER

Is not amorous a good word?   60

Enter TRAPDOOR *like a poor soldier with a patch o'er one eye, and*
TEARCAT *with him, all tatters*

TRAPDOOR

Shall we set upon the infantry, these troops of foot? Zounds,
yonder comes Moll, my whorish master and mistress, would
I had her kidneys between my teeth.

TEARCAT

I had rather have a cow-heel.

TRAPDOOR

Zounds, I am so patched up, she cannot discover me: we'll   65
on.

---

53 *Pimlico* cf. IV.ii, 12
54 *nappy* heady, intoxicated
55 *ging* company
64 *cow-heel* the foot of a cow or ox stewed to form a jelly

---

54 *boon voyage*. The phrase, like others, was commonly anglicized.
54 *spice-cakes*. In Glapthorne's *Lady Mother* of 1635, III.ii (qu. Sugden
    s.v. Pimlico), one character reminds another of walking to Pimlico 'to
    eat plumcakes and cream'.
56 *the world's end*. There was more than one tavern of this name then at
    some considerable distance from London.

TEARCAT

Alla corago then.

TRAPDOOR

Good your honours and worships, enlarge the ears of
commiseration, and let the sound of a hoarse military organ-
pipe penetrate your pitiful bowels to extract out of them so   70
many small drops of silver as may give a hard straw-bed
lodging to a couple of maimed soldiers.

JACK DAPPER

Where are you maimed?

TEARCAT

In both our nether limbs.

MOLL

Come, come, Dapper, let's give 'em something: 'las poor   75
men, what money have you? by my troth I love a soldier with
my soul.

SIR BEAUTEOUS

Stay, stay, where have you served?

SIR THOMAS

In any part of the Low Countries?

TRAPDOOR

Not in the Low Countries, if it please your manhood, but in   80
Hungary against the Turk at the siege of Belgrade.

LORD NOLAND

Who served there with you, sirrah?

TRAPDOOR

Many Hungarians, Moldavians, Walachians, and Transyl-
vanians, with some Sclavonians, and retiring home, sir, the

---

67 *Alla corago* a corruption of the Italian *coraggio*

75 s.p. MOLL. This speech should perhaps be given to Lord Noland: it is
hardly characteristic of Moll, who spies out the rogues a few lines later,
and it is not difficult to see how *L.Nol.* or *Nol.* could be misread as *Mol*
(her normal speech-prefix).

81 *the siege of Belgrade.* Belgrade has had numerous sieges, the most
famous of which, that of 1455–56, raised by the great János Hunyadi,
seems to have been the last before 1611; from 1521 to 1688 the city
remained in the hands of the Turks. There was, however, constant
warfare in Hungary throughout this time, and perhaps Trapdoor has
muddled memories of the so-called 'Long War' (1593–1606), a confused
and often bitter, partly religious struggle involving, as well as the
Emperor's native Hungarians and the Turks, all the nationalities mentioned in the next speech. (In *A Fair Quarrel*, IV.i, 33, we hear of
roaring in Sclavonian, along with other more obviously Londonian
dialects.)

Venetian galleys took us prisoners, yet freed us, and suffered   85
us to beg up and down the country.

JACK DAPPER

You have ambled all over Italy then?

TRAPDOOR

Oh sir, from Venice to Roma, Vecchio, Bononia, Romania,
Bolonia, Modena, Piacenza, and Tuscana with all her cities,
as Pistoia, Valteria, Mountepulchena, Arezzo, with the   90
Siennois, and diverse others.

MOLL

Mere rogues, put spurs to 'em once more.

JACK DAPPER

Thou look'st like a strange creature, a fat butter-box, yet
speak'st English. —What art thou?

TEARCAT

Ick, mine Here? Ick bin den ruffling Tearcat, den brave Soldado,   95
ick bin dorick all Dutchlant gueresen: der Shellum das meere ine
Beasa ine Woert gaeb. Ick slaag um stroakes on tom Cop: dastick
den hundred touzun Divell halle, frollick mine Here.

SIR BEAUTEOUS

Here, here, let's be rid of their jobbering.

MOLL

Not a cross, Sir Beauteous. You base rogues, I have taken   100

---

93 *butter-box* contemptuous term for a Dutchman
99 *jobbering* jabbering

88–91 An amble indeed: Vecchio is presumably Civitavecchia, Bononia
and Bolonia are one and the same, the modern Bologna, Romania is
Romagna, Valteria Volterra, Mountepulchena Montepulciano. Moll
recognizes that this is no proper journey but a string of names picked
up at hearsay.

95–8 This piece of bastard Dutch is spelt here exactly as in Q (where it is
printed in black letter), though the punctuation has been regularized. A
'translation' must be a matter partly of guesswork, but it isn't entirely
gibberish, though some words are hard to identify. (I have supposed
that, since Tearcat goes once into Spanish, he may also include an
attempt at a French word: it looks as if *Beasa* may be *baiser*.) 'I, sir?
I am the ruffling Tearcat, the brave soldier, I have travelled through all
Holland: the rascal who gave more [than] a kiss and a word. I beat him
with blows on the head; pulled out thence a hundred thousand devils,
cheerfully, sir'. To ruffle is to swagger, also to handle a woman with
rude familiarity; for the cant use, see below, l. 145 and Appendix.

100 *Not a cross.* From the fourteenth century at latest coins were frequently
stamped with a cross on the reverse side: Sir Beauteous has made to get
rid of them by offering money.

measure of you better than a tailor can, and I'll fit you as you,
monster with one eye, have fitted me.

TRAPDOOR

Your worship will not abuse a soldier.

MOLL

Soldier? thou deservest to be hanged up by that tongue which
dishonours so noble a profession: soldier, you skeldering   105
varlet? Hold, stand, there should be a trapdoor hereabouts.

Pull off his patch

TRAPDOOR

The balls of these glaziers of mine, mine eyes, shall be shot
up and down in any hot piece of service for my invincible
mistress.

JACK DAPPER

I did not think there had been such knavery in black patches   110
as now I see.

MOLL

Oh sir, he hath been brought up in the Isle of Dogs, and can
both fawn like a spaniel and bite like a mastiff, as he finds
occasion.

LORD NOLAND

What are you, sirrah? a bird of this feather too?   115

TEARCAT

A man beaten from the wars, sir.

SIR THOMAS

I think so, for you never stood to fight.

---

101 *fit* in the sense of 'provide for', as well as literally
107 *glaziers* cant term for eyes

---

105 *skeldering*. Sponging: the term seems to have been used especially of
vagabonds begging under the guise of old soldiers: cf. Jonson, *Every
Man Out Of His Humour*, the Characters (description of Shift): 'A
threadbare shark; one that never was a soldier, yet lives upon lendings.
His profession is skeldering and odling'. See *Lanthorn and Candlelight*,
xxiv, for a description of their methods of begging.
110 *black patches*. They were worn as ornaments by ladies and fops.
112 *the Isle of Dogs*. The peninsula on the north bank of the Thames
opposite Greenwich: according to Stow it took its name from hunting
dogs being kennelled there when Greenwich was a royal palace. It had
become a place of refuge for debtors and criminals; the name gave rise
to frequent jokes of this kind. In 1598 the performance of a now lost
play by Nashe and Jonson called *The Isle of Dogs* led to the theatres
being closed for two months. In *The Return of Parnassus*, part 2, one of
the students retires to the Isle of Dogs to become a professional satirist.

JACK DAPPER

What's thy name, fellow soldier?

TEARCAT

I am called by those that have seen my valour, Tearcat.

OMNES

Tearcat?   120

MOLL

A mere whip-jack, and that is, in the commonwealth of
rogues, a slave that can talk of sea-fight, name all your chief
pirates, discover more countries to you than either the Dutch,
Spanish, French, or English ever found out, yet indeed all
his service is by land, and that is to rob a fair, or some such   125
venturous exploit; Tearcat, foot sirrah, I have your name,
now I remember me, in my book of horners, horns for the
thumb, you know how.

TEARCAT

No indeed, Captain Moll (for I know you by sight), I am no
such nipping Christian, but a maunderer upon the pad, I   130
confess; and meeting with honest Trapdoor here, whom
you had cashiered from bearing arms, out at elbows under
your colours, I instructed him in the rudiments of roguery,
and by my map made him sail over any country you can
name so that now he can maunder better than myself.   135

JACK DAPPER

So then, Trapdoor, thou art turned soldier now.

TRAPDOOR

Alas sir, now there's no wars, 'tis the safest course of life I
could take.

MOLL

I hope then you can cant, for by your cudgels, you, sirrah,
are an upright man.   140

---

121 *whip-jack* a vagabond who pretends to be a distressed sailor: there
   is a similar description in Dekker's *Bellman of London*
130 *nipping* thieving
130 *maunderer upon the pad* beggar on the highway; so *maunder* beg
140 *upright man*, etc. see Appendix

127-8 *horns for the thumb.* A horn-thumb was a thimble of horn used by
   cutpurses for protecting the thumb against the edge of the knife used in
   cutting the purse-strings; hence used of pickpockets themselves.
139 *you can cant.* You have learnt all the appropriate specialist slang. For an
   explanation of the cant terms used in this scene, see the glossary given
   in the Appendix, and, generally, the various early authorities there
   cited.

TRAPDOOR

As any walks the highway, I assure you.

MOLL

And Tearcat, what are you? a wild rogue, an angler, or a
ruffler?

TEARCAT

Brother to this upright man, flesh and blood, ruffling Tearcat
is my name, and a ruffler is my style, my title, my profession.   145

MOLL

Sirrah, where's your doxy? halt not with me.

OMNES

Doxy, Moll, what's that?

MOLL

His wench.

TRAPDOOR

My doxy? I have by the salomon a doxy, that carries a
kinchin mort in her slate at her back, besides my dell and my   150
dainty wild dell, with all whom I'll tumble this next darkmans in the strommel, and drink ben booze, and eat a fat
gruntling cheat, a cackling cheat, and a quacking cheat.

JACK DAPPER

Here's old cheating.

TRAPDOOR

My doxy stays for me in a boozing ken, brave captain.   155

MOLL

He says his wench stays for him in an alehouse: you are no
pure rogues.

TEARCAT

Pure rogues? no, we scorn to be pure rogues, but if you
come to our lib ken, or our stalling ken, you shall find neither
him nor me a queer cuffin.   160

MOLL

So sir, no churl of you?

TEARCAT

No, but a ben cove, a brave cove, a gentry cuffin.

146 *halt not* don't limp, i.e., don't be roundabout or devious
150 *slate* see Appendix   154 *old* fine, rare

151–3 i.e., I'll tumble this next night in the straw, and drink good booze, and
    eat a fat pig, a capon, and a duck. For *booze* Q has *baufe*, which is
    evidently a misprint for *bouse* or *bowse*. See further in the Appendix.
156–7 *you are no pure rogues*. Bullen takes this to be ironical; but Moll may
    mean pure in the sense of sexually pure or chaste, and that is certainly
    the sense in which Tearcat picks up the word.

LORD NOLAND
   Call you this canting?
JACK DAPPER
   Zounds, I'll give a schoolmaster half a crown a week, and
   teach me this pedlar's French.   165
TRAPDOOR
   Do but stroll, sir, half a harvest with us, sir, and you shall
   gabble your bellyful.
MOLL
   Come you rogue, cant with me.
SIR THOMAS
   Well said, Moll, cant with her, sirrah, and you shall have
   money, else not a penny.   170
TRAPDOOR
   I'll have a bout if she please.
MOLL
   Come on sirrah.
TRAPDOOR
   Ben mort, shall you and I heave a booth, mill a ken, or nip a
   bung? And then we'll couch a hogshead under the ruffmans,
   and there you shall wap with me, and I'll niggle with you.   175
MOLL
   Out, you damned impudent rascal.
TRAPDOOR
   Cut benar whids, and hold your fambles and your stamps.
LORD NOLAND
   Nay, nay, Moll, why art thou angry? what was his gibberish?
MOLL
   Marry, this, my Lord, says he: Ben mort (good wench), shall
   you and I heave a booth, mill a ken, or nip a bung? shall you 180
   and I rob a house, or cut a purse?
OMNES
   Very good.
MOLL
   And then we'll couch a hogshead under the ruffmans: and
   then we'll lie under a hedge.
TRAPDOOR
   That was my desire, Captain, as 'tis fit a soldier should lie. 185

177 *Cut benar whids, and hold your fambles and your stamps* speak
   better words, and hold your hands and your feet

165 *pedlar's French.* 'Canting language to be found among none but beggars'
   (*Bellman of London*); also applied generally to unintelligible jargon.
   Pedlars were widely regarded as inescapably dishonest.

MOLL

And there you shall wap with me, and I'll niggle with you,
and that's all.

SIR BEAUTEOUS

Nay, nay, Moll, what's that wap?

JACK DAPPER

Nay teach me what niggling is, I'd fain be niggling.

MOLL

Wapping and niggling is all one, the rogue my man can tell   190
you.

TRAPDOOR

'Tis fadoodling, if it please you.

SIR BEAUTEOUS

This is excellent, one fit more, good Moll.

MOLL

Come you rogue, sing with me.
      A gage of ben rom-booze   *The song*   195
      In a boozing ken of Rom-ville

---

193 *fit* strain or bout

---

192 *fadoodling*. *OED* has nothing earlier than 1670 for 'fadoodle', when it
    meant something ridiculous; but as Reed remarks, the explanation is
    evident from Trapdoor's use of it.

194ff. s.p. ed. In Q there is no speech-heading following Moll's invitation
    until the third line of the song, where *T.Cat* is prefixed. At the sixth
    line *The song* appears in the right-hand margin, where a chorus is
    strongly suggested. *T.Cat* is again prefixed to the tenth line; the last
    two lines seem again to be a chorus. The song, translated with the help
    of *Lanthorn and Candlelight*, means:

> A quart pot of good wine
> In an alehouse of London
> Is better than a cloak,
> Meat, bread, whey, or pottage,
> Which we steal in the country.
> Oh I would lie all the day,
> Oh I would lie all the night,
> By the mass, under the bushes,
> By the mass, in the stocks.
> And wear bolts (or fetters)
> And sleep till a tramp lay with my wench,
> So my boozy head might drink wine well.
> Away to the highway, let us go,
> Away to the highway, let us go.

See Appendix for Dekker's definitions, and Moll's paraphrase at l. 234.

TEARCAT   Is benar than a caster,
          Peck, pennam, lap or popler,
          Which we mill in deuse a vill.
BOTH   Oh I would lib all the lightmans,   200
          Oh I would lib all the darkmans,
          By the salomon, under the ruffmans,
          By the salomon, in the hartmans.
TEARCAT   And scour the queer cramp-ring,
          And couch till a palliard docked my dell,   205
          So my boozy nab might skew rom-booze well.
BOTH   Avast to the pad, let us bing,
          Avast to the pad, let us bing.
OMNES
    Fine knaves i'faith.
JACK DAPPER
    The grating of ten new cartwheels, and the gruntling of five   210
    hundred hogs coming from Romford market, cannot make a
    worse noise than this canting language does in my ears; pray,
    my Lord Noland, let's give these soldiers their pay.
SIR BEAUTEOUS
    Agreed, and let them march.
LORD NOLAND
    Here, Moll.   215
MOLL
    Now I see that you are stalled to the rogue, and are not
    ashamed of your professions, look you: my Lord Noland
    here and these gentlemen bestows upon you two, two
    bordes and a half, that's two shillings sixpence.
TRAPDOOR
    Thanks to your lordship.   220
TEARCAT
    Thanks, heroical captain.
MOLL
    Away.
TRAPDOOR
    We shall cut ben whids of your masters and mistress-ship,
    wheresoever we come.

198 *lap* ed. (lay Q)   199 *vill* ed. (vile Q)
204 *cramp-ring* handcuffs, a cant adaptation of the standard word (cf.
    IV.ii, 16)
219 *bordes* shillings   223 *cut ben whids* speak well

211 *Romford market.* Romford had an important market, and allusions to
    Romford hogs are frequent. cf., e.g., *A Chaste Maid*, IV.i, 98.

MOLL

You'll maintain, sirrah, the old justice's plot to his face?   225

TRAPDOOR

Else trine me on the cheats: hang me.

MOLL

Be sure you meet me there.

TRAPDOOR

Without any more maundering I'll do't: follow, brave
Tearcat.

TEARCAT

I prae, sequor; let us go, mouse.   230

Exeunt they two, manet the rest

LORD NOLAND

Moll, what was in that canting song?

MOLL

Troth my Lord, only a praise of good drink, the only milk
which these wild beasts love to suck, and thus it was:

> A rich cup of wine,
> Oh it is juice divine,   235
> More wholesome for the head
> Than meat, drink, or bread;
> To fill my drunken pate
> With that, I'd sit up late,
> By the heels would I lie,   240
> Under a lousy hedge die,
> Let a slave have a pull
> At my whore, so I be full
> Of that precious liquor

—and a parcel of such stuff, my Lord, not worth the opening.   245

Enter a CUTPURSE *very gallant, with four or five men after him,
one with a wand*

LORD NOLAND

What gallant comes yonder?

SIR THOMAS

Mass, I think I know him, 'tis one of Cumberland.

---

226 *trine me on the cheats* hang me on the gallows; but cf. Appendix
230 *I prae, sequor* go before, I follow
245 s.d. *gallant* finely dressed

---

228 *maundering.* Probably chattering; i.e., without more ado. The word is
apparently distinct from that used above at l. 130; but cf. Appendix.

1 CUTPURSE
   Shall we venture to shuffle in amongst yon heap of gallants
   and strike?
2 CUTPURSE
   'Tis a question whether there be any silver shells amongst   250
   them for all their satin outsides.
OMNES [CUTPURSES]
   Let's try.
MOLL
   Pox on him, a gallant? Shadow me, I know him: 'tis one that
   cumbers the land indeed; if he swim near to the shore of any
   of your pockets, look to your purses.   255
OMNES
   Is't possible?
MOLL
   This brave fellow is no better than a foist.
OMNES
   Foist, what's that?
MOLL
   A diver with two fingers, a pickpocket; all his train study the
   figging-law, that's to say cutting of purses and foisting; one   260
   of them is a nip, I took him once i'the twopenny gallery at
   the Fortune; then there's a cloyer, or snap, that dogs any
   new brother in that trade, and snaps will have half in any
   booty; he with the wand is both a stale, whose office is to
   face a man i'the streets, whilst shells are drawn by another,   265
   and then with his black conjuring rod in his hand, he, by the
   nimbleness of his eye and juggling-stick, will, in cheaping a
   piece of plate at a goldsmith's stall, make four or five rings
   mount from the top of his caduceus, and as if it were at leap-
   frog, they skip into his hand presently.   270

249 *strike* steal; to strike a hand is to do a job (*Lanthorn and Candle-
       light*, xxiv)
250 *shells* money   253 *Shadow me* follow me closely
256 s.p. OMNES i.e., Moll's companions
257 *foist* etc. see Appendix   267 *cheaping* bargaining for

---

261–2 *the twopenny gallery at the Fortune.* Not quite the cheapest place, for
    one could get in for a penny. The Fortune (see note to title-page,
    p. 2) was the theatre in which *The Roaring Girl* was then being per-
    formed.
269 *caduceus.* Strictly a herald's wand: I am not sure whether Moll is
    referring again to the cutpurse's stick used like a curb, or to a baton on
    which the goldsmith might keep rings for sale. Mercury carried a
    caduceus, and 'mercury' meant in popular usage a dexterous thief.

2 CUTPURSE
Zounds, we are smoked.
OMNES [CUTPURSES]
Ha?
2 CUTPURSE
We are boiled, pox on her; see, Moll, the roaring drab.
1 CUTPURSE
All the diseases of sixteen hospitals boil her! Away.
MOLL
Bless you, sir.   275
1 CUTPURSE
And you, good sir.
MOLL
Dost not ken me, man?
1 CUTPURSE
No, trust me, sir.
MOLL
Heart, there's a knight to whom I'm bound for many
favours lost his purse at the last new play i'the 'Swan, seven   280
angels in't: make it good, you're best; do you see? no more.
1 CUTPURSE
A synagogue shall be called, Mistress Mary, disgrace me
not; pacus palabros, I will conjure for you, farewell.
                                        [*Exeunt* CUTPURSES]
MOLL
Did not I tell you, my Lord?
LORD NOLAND
I wonder how thou camest to the knowledge of these nasty   285
villains.
SIR THOMAS
And why do the foul mouths of the world call thee Moll
Cutpurse? a name, methinks, damned and odious.
MOLL
Dare any step forth to my face and say,
'I have ta'en thee doing so, Moll'? I must confess,   290

278   *trust* ed. (rrust Q)
280   *Swan* the theatre on Bankside near the Globe
282   *synagogue* presumably an assembly of thieves to get the money
       together
283   *pacus palabros* a corruption of Spanish *pocas palabras*, few words.
       cf. *The Taming of the Shrew*, Ind. i, 5

279ff. This episode seems to be based on an established custom of Mary
        Frith's: see above, p. xvi.

In younger days, when I was apt to stray,
I have sat amongst such adders; seen their stings,
As any here might, and in full playhouses
Watched their quick-diving hands, to bring to shame
Such rogues, and in that stream met an ill name: 295
When next, my Lord, you spy any one of those,
So he be in his art a scholar, question him,
Tempt him with gold to open the large book
Of his close villainies: and you yourself shall cant
Better than poor Moll can, and know more laws   300
Of cheators, lifters, nips, foists, puggards, curbers,
With all the devil's black guard, than it is fit
Should be discovered to a noble wit.
I know they have their orders, offices,
Circuits and circles, unto which they are bound,   305
To raise their own damnation in.
JACK DAPPER   How dost thou know it?
MOLL
    As you do, I show it you, they to me show it.
    Suppose, my Lord, you were in Venice.
LORD NOLAND   Well.
MOLL
    If some Italian pander there would tell
    All the close tricks of courtesans, would not you   310
    Hearken to such a fellow?
LORD NOLAND   Yes.
MOLL   And here,
    Being come from Venice, to a friend most dear
    That were to travel thither, you would proclaim
    Your knowledge in those villainies, to save
    Your friend from their quick danger: must you have   315

---

301 *cheators* or fingerers, those who win money by false dice: see
     Appendix
301 *lifters* thieves (an old usage revived in 'shop-lifters')
301 *nips* etc. see Appendix
306 *raise . . . in* make more complete (literally to fatten)
315 *quick* lively

---

301 *puggards*. Thieves: seemingly a unique occurrence, though cf. *The
     Winter's Tale*, IV.iii, 7, for *pugging*. It is possible that we should read
     'priggard', a word which in one form or another often occurs for thief.
302 *black guard*. A guard of attendants, black in person, dress, or character:
     cf. *Lanthorn and Candlelight*, ii: 'The great Lord of Limbo did therefore
     command all his Black Guard . . . to bestir them'.

A black ill name, because ill things you know?
Good troth my Lord, I am made Moll Cutpurse so.
How many are whores in small ruffs and still looks!
How many chaste, whose names fill slander's books!
Were all men cuckolds, whom gallants in their scorns　　　320
Call so, we should not walk for goring horns.
Perhaps for my mad going some reprove me,
I please myself, and care not else who love me.

OMNES

A brave mind, Moll, i'faith.

SIR THOMAS

Come my Lord, shall's to the ordinary?　　　325

LORD NOLAND

Ay, 'tis noon sure.

MOLL

Good my Lord, let not my name condemn me to you or to
the world: a fencer I hope may be called a coward, is he so for
that? If all that have ill names in London were to be whipped,
and to pay but twelve-pence apiece to the beadle, I would　　330
rather have his office than a constable's.

JACK DAPPER

So would I, Captain Moll: 'twere a sweet tickling office
i'faith.　　　　　　　　　　　　　　　　　　　　*Exeunt*

[Act V, Scene ii]

Enter SIR ALEXANDER WENGRAVE, GOSHAWK *and* GREENWIT,
and others

SIR ALEXANDER

My son marry a thief, that impudent girl,
Whom all the world stick their worst eyes upon?

GREENWIT

How will your care prevent it?

GOSHAWK　　　　　　　　　　　'Tis impossible.
They marry close, they're gone, but none knows whither.

SIR ALEXANDER

Oh gentlemen, when has a father's heart-strings　　　5
Held out so long from breaking?

---

323 *love* ed. (loves Q)
332 *tickling* diverting, but 'tickler' was also slang for a whip
332f. prose ed. (rough verse Q)
　4 *close* secretly

Enter a SERVANT

Now what news, sir?

SERVANT
They were met upo'th'water an hour since, sir,
Putting in towards the Sluice.

SIR ALEXANDER The Sluice? come gentlemen,
[*Exit* SERVANT]

'Tis Lambeth works against us.

GREENWIT And that Lambeth
Joins more mad matches than your six wet towns, 10
'Twixt that and Windsor Bridge, where fares lie soaking.

SIR ALEXANDER
Delay no time, sweet gentlemen: to Blackfriars,
We'll take a pair of oars and make after 'em.

Enter TRAPDOOR

TRAPDOOR
Your son, and that bold masculine ramp
My mistress, are landed now at Tower.

SIR ALEXANDER Hoyda, at Tower? 15

TRAPDOOR
I heard it now reported. [*Exit* TRAPDOOR]

SIR ALEXANDER Which way, gentlemen,
Shall I bestow my care? I'm drawn in pieces
Betwixt deceit and shame.

Enter SIR [GUY] FITZ-ALLARD

---

12 *to Blackfriars* i.e., they will take a boat from Blackfriars Stairs and
   cross to Lambeth
14 *ramp* cf. III.iii, 7

---

8 *the Sluice.* The Sluice was an embankment built to protect the low-
   lying area of Lambeth Marsh from inundations; it was used as a landing-
   place. Perhaps we are meant also to think of the verb to sluice (= to
   copulate with).
9 *Lambeth* was also renowned as the haunt of thieves, etc.; but there is
   perhaps an allusion to the boat-building works there; additionally
   Lambeth was the place from which (after crossing the river by boat) one
   would set out towards the south-west.
10 *your six wet* (i.e., riverside) *towns.* A note in Reed's edition of Dodsley
   suggests that the six are Fulham, Richmond, Kingston, Hampton,
   Chertsey, and Staines.
11 *where fares lie soaking.* In more recent centuries, to soak can mean to
   linger over sexual intercourse; and the whole phrase suggests the use of
   the riverside towns for sexual excursions.

SIR GUY   Sir Alexander,
　You're well met, and most rightly served:
　My daughter was a scorn to you.
SIR ALEXANDER   Say not so, sir.   20
SIR GUY
　A very abject she, poor gentlewoman.
　Your house has been dishonoured: give you joy, sir,
　Of your son's gaskin-bride, you'll be a grandfather shortly
　To a fine crew of roaring sons and daughters,
　'Twill help to stock the suburbs passing well, sir.   25
SIR ALEXANDER
　Oh play not with the miseries of my heart.
　Wounds should be dressed and healed, not vexed, or left
　Wide open, to the anguish of the patient,
　And scornful air let in: rather let pity
　And advice charitably help to refresh 'em.   30
SIR GUY
　Who'd place his charity so unworthily,
　Like one that gives alms to a cursing beggar?
　Had I but found one spark of goodness in you
　Toward my deserving child, which then grew fond
　Of your son's virtues, I had eased you now.   35
　But I perceive both fire of youth and goodness
　Are raked up in the ashes of your age,
　Else no such shame should have come near your house,
　Nor such ignoble sorrow touch your heart.
SIR ALEXANDER
　If not for worth, for pity's sake assist me.   40
GREENWIT
　You urge a thing past sense, how can he help you?
　All his assistance is as frail as ours,
　Full as uncertain where's the place that holds 'em.

---

21 *abject* is here a noun   22 *has* ed. (had Q)
37 *raked up* i.e., smothered

---

23 *gaskin-bride.* One, that is, wearing gaskins or loose breeches: the Q
　spelling is Gaskoyne, which indicates a popular and possibly correct
　etymology (i.e., from Gascony).
25 *The suburbs* were notoriously corrupt, licentious, and full of brothels.
　cf. Nashe, *Christ's Tears over Jerusalem* (Works [1904], II, 148): 'Lon-
　don, what are thy suburbs but licensed stews?' But those living in the
　suburbs would be penniless too: cf. *Lanthorn and Candlelight*, ix:
　'these suburb sinners have no land to live upon but their legs'. A.
　suburb-sinner was a prostitute. And see the Prologus to this play, l. 21.

One brings us water-news; then comes another
With a full-charged mouth, like a culverin's voice,   45
And he reports the Tower: whose sounds are truest?
GOSHAWK
In vain you flatter him, Sir Alexander.
SIR ALEXANDER
I flatter him? Gentlemen, you wrong me grossly.
GREENWIT
He does it well i'faith.
SIR GUY   Both news are false,
Of Tower or water: they took no such way yet.   50
SIR ALEXANDER
Oh strange: hear you this, gentlemen, yet more plunges?
SIR GUY
They're nearer than you think for, yet more close
Than if they were further off.
SIR ALEXANDER   How am I lost
In these distractions?
SIR GUY   For your speeches, gentlemen,
In taxing me for rashness, 'fore you all   55
I will engage my state to half his wealth,
Nay to his son's revenues, which are less,
And yet nothing at all till they come from him,
That I could (if my will stuck to my power)
Prevent this marriage yet, nay banish her   60
Forever from his thoughts, much more his arms.
SIR ALEXANDER
Slack not this goodness, though you heap upon me

45 *culverin* a large cannon
51 *plunges* dilemmas; cf. IV.i, 152
52 *close* secret, hidden
54–5 'Though I foresee that you will tax me with rashness'
56 *engage* wager
   his i.e., Sir Alexander's
59 *if my will stuck to my power* if I would do what I could

48 s.p. SIR ALEXANDER ed. (Fitz-All. Q) I take it that Goshawk means
   flatter in the sense of coax or wheedle, but Sir Alexander mistakes this
   for the common use. If Q is correct, presumably Goshawk is being
   ironic: one must then, with previous editors, punctuate his speech
   '. . . flatter him. Sir Alexander—', as if he were going to explain why
   'flattery' will get him nowhere; but there seems no reason why such
   a speech should come at this point.
49 Does this mean that Goshawk and Greenwit are in the Fitz-Allard
   plot? cf. l. 92.

Mountains of malice and revenge hereafter:
I'd willingly resign up half my state to him,
So he would marry the meanest drudge I hire.   65
GREENWIT
He talks impossibilities, and you believe 'em.
SIR GUY
I talk no more than I know how to finish,
My fortunes else are his that dares stake with me.
The poor young gentleman I love and pity,
And to keep shame from him (because the spring   70
Of his affection was my daughter's first,
Till his frown blasted all), do but estate him
In those possessions which your love and care
Once pointed out for him, that he may have room
To entertain fortunes of noble birth,   75
Where now his desperate wants casts him upon her:
And if I do not, for his own sake chiefly,
Rid him of this disease that now grows on him,
I'll forfeit my whole state, before these gentlemen.
GREENWIT
Troth but you shall not undertake such matches,   80
We'll persuade so much with you.
SIR ALEXANDER   Here's my ring,
He will believe this token: 'fore these gentlemen
I will confirm it fully: all those lands
My first love 'lotted him, he shall straight possess
In that refusal.
SIR GUY   If I change it not,   85
Change me into a beggar.
GREENWIT   Are you mad, sir?
SIR GUY
'Tis done.
GOSHAWK   Will you undo yourself by doing,
And show a prodigal trick in your old days?
SIR ALEXANDER
'Tis a match, gentlemen.

70–1 'Because the fountain of his love belonged first to my daughter'
72 *his* sc. Sir Alexander's
76 *her* sc. Moll   80 *matches* wagers
85 *In that refusal* i.e., in refusing Moll

64 An example of the slapdash versification of which there is much in this
   play: the line seems to be emphatically a pentameter with another foot
   limping in at the end.

SIR GUY   Ay, ay, sir, ay.
　I ask no favour, trust to you for none,   90
　My hope rests in the goodness of your son.

　　　　　　　　　　　　　　　　Exit FITZ-ALLARD

GREENWIT
　He holds it up well yet.
GOSHAWK   Of an old knight i'faith.
SIR ALEXANDER
　Cursed be the time I laid his first love barren,
　Wilfully barren, that before this hour
　Had sprung forth fruits of comfort and of honour;   95
　He loved a virtuous gentlewoman.

　　　　　　　　　Enter MOLL [*in male dress*]

GOSHAWK   Life,
　Here's Moll.
GREENWIT   Jack?
GOSHAWK   How dost thou, Jack?
MOLL   How dost thou,
　　　　　　　　　　　　　　　　　　gallant?

SIR ALEXANDER
　Impudence, where's my son?
MOLL   Weakness, go look him.
SIR ALEXANDER
　Is this your wedding gown?
MOLL   The man talks monthly:
　Hot broth and a dark chamber for the knight,   100
　I see he'll be stark mad at our next meeting.   *Exit* MOLL
GOSHAWK
　Why sir, take comfort now, there's no such matter.
　No priest will marry her, sir, for a woman
　Whiles that shape's on, and it was never known
　Two men were married and conjoined in one: 105
　Your son hath made some shift to love another.

---

92 *Of* in the true manner of

---

99 *The man talks monthly*. i.e., madly (as if under the influence of the
　moon). cf. *Lanthorn and Candlelight*, viii: 'A moon-man signifies in
　English a "madman" because the moon hath greatest domination above
　any other planet over the bodies of frantic persons'.
103 *No priest will marry her . . . for a woman*. 'Marriages' between two men
　crop up in several plays, e.g., Fletcher's *Wild Goose Chase* and *Mon-
　sieur Thomas*.

SIR ALEXANDER
Whate'er she be, she has my blessing with her,
May they be rich, and fruitful, and receive
Like comfort to their issue as I take
In them. Has pleased me now: marrying not this,   110
Through a whole world he could not choose amiss.
GREENWIT
Glad y'are so penitent for your former sin, sir.
GOSHAWK
Say he should take a wench with her smock-dowry,
No portion with her but her lips and arms?
SIR ALEXANDER
Why, who thrive better, sir? they have most blessing,   115
Though other have more wealth, and least repent:
Many that want most know the most content.
GREENWIT
Say he should marry a kind youthful sinner?
SIR ALEXANDER
Age will quench that,
Any offence but theft and drunkenness,   120
Nothing but death can wipe away:
Their sins are green even when their heads are grey.
Nay I despair not now, my heart's cheered, gentlemen,
No face can come unfortunately to me.

Enter a SERVANT

Now sir, your news?
SERVANT   Your son with his fair bride   125
Is near at hand.
SIR ALEXANDER   Fair may their fortunes be.

---

118 *kind* winsome

---

113 *with her smock-dowry.* i.e., with no dowry but her smock: apparently a
unique occurrence, but cf. *A Chaste Maid*, III.iii, 77: 'I took her with
one smock', and *A Trick to Catch the Old One*, IV.iv, 8: 'She's worth
four hundred a year in her very smock'.

119–21 stet Q (except for lineation, Q making a single line from *Age* to
drunkenness). The sense is obscure as the sentence stands, and faulty
lineation suggests that there may be corruption. Possibly we should
read (l. 121) 'And these nothing but death can wipe away'—or some
such phrase.

GREENWIT
  Now you're resolved, sir, it was never she?
SIR ALEXANDER
  I find it in the music of my heart.

Enter MOLL *masked, in* SEBASTIAN's *hand, and* FITZ-ALLARD

  See where they come.
GOSHAWK   A proper lusty presence, sir.
SIR ALEXANDER
  Now has he pleased me right, I always counselled him   130
  To choose a goodly personable creature,
  Just of her pitch was my first wife his mother.
SEBASTIAN
  Before I dare discover my offence,
  I kneel for pardon.
SIR ALEXANDER   My heart gave it thee
  Before thy tongue could ask it: 135
  Rise, thou hast raised my joy to greater height
  Than to that seat where grief dejected it:
  Both welcome to my love and care for ever.
  Hide not my happiness too long, all's pardoned,
  Here are our friends, salute her, gentlemen.   140
                          They unmask her
OMNES
  Heart, who's this? Moll!
SIR ALEXANDER
  Oh my reviving shame, is't I must live
  To be struck blind? be it the work of sorrow,
  Before age take't in hand.
SIR GUY   Darkness and death.
  Have you deceived me thus? did I engage   145
  My whole estate for this?
SIR ALEXANDER   You asked no favour,
  And you shall find as little; since my comforts
  Play false with me, I'll be as cruel to thee
  As grief to fathers' hearts.
MOLL   Why, what's the matter with you,
  'Less too much joy should make your age forgetful?   150
  Are you too well, too happy?
SIR ALEXANDER   With a vengeance.

127 *resolved* persuaded
141 *who's this? Moll!* ed. (who this *Mol*? Q)
150 *Less* unless

MOLL

    Methinks you should be proud of such a daughter,

    As good a man as your son.

SIR ALEXANDER   Oh monstrous impudence.

MOLL

    You had no note before, an unmarked knight,

    Now all the town will take regard on you,   155

    And all your enemies fear you for my sake:

    You may pass where you list, through crowds most thick,

    And come off bravely with your purse unpicked.

    You do not know the benefits I bring with me:

    No cheat dares work upon you with thumb or knife,   160

    While y'ave a roaring girl to your son's wife.

SIR ALEXANDER

    A devil rampant.

SIR GUY   Have you so much charity

    Yet to release me of my last rash bargain,

    And I'll give in your pledge?

SIR ALEXANDER   No sir, I stand to't,

    I'll work upon advantage, as all mischiefs   165

    Do upon me.

SIR GUY   Content: bear witness all then,

    His are the lands, and so contention ends.

    Here comes your son's bride, 'twixt two noble friends.

Enter the LORD NOLAND, *and* SIR BEAUTEOUS GANYMEDE, *with*
MARY FITZ-ALLARD *between them, the* CITIZENS *and their* WIVES
with them

MOLL

    Now are you gulled as you would be: thank me for't,

    I'd a forefinger in't.

SEBASTIAN   Forgive me, father: 170

    Though there before your eyes my sorrow feigned,

    This still was she for whom true love complained.

SIR ALEXANDER

    Blessings eternal and the joys of angels

    Begin your peace here, to be signed in heaven!

154 *unmarked* unnoticed, of no account
160 *cheat* in the general sense of pickpocket or cutpurse
    thumb cf. V.i, 128
165 *work upon advantage* take advantage of my position (unscrupul-
    ously): cf. *A Fair Quarrel*, III.iii, 151

169 *forefinger.* Despite Moll's skill with instruments we should probably
resist a sexual innuendo here.

How short my sleep of sorrow seems now to me,   175
To this eternity of boundless comforts,
That finds no want but utterance and expression.
My Lord, your office here appears so honourably,
So full of ancient goodness, grace, and worthiness,
I never took more joy in sight of man   180
Than in your comfortable presence now.

LORD NOLAND
Nor I more delight in doing grace to virtue,
Than in this worthy gentlewoman, your son's bride,
Noble Fitz-Allard's daughter, to whose honour
And modest fame I am a servant vowed,   185
So is this knight.

SIR ALEXANDER   Your loves make my joys proud.
Bring forth those deeds of land my care laid ready,
And which, old knight, thy nobleness may challenge,
Joined with thy daughter's virtues, whom I prize now
As dearly as that flesh I call mine own.   190
Forgive me, worthy gentlewoman, 'twas my blindness:
When I rejected thee, I saw thee not,
Sorrow and wilful rashness grew like films
Over the eyes of judgment; now so clear
I see the brightness of thy worth appear.   195

MARY
Duty and love may I deserve in those,
And all my wishes have a perfect close.

SIX ALEXANDER
That tongue can never err, the sound's so sweet.
Here, honest son, receive into thy hands
The keys of wealth, possession of those lands   200
Which my first care provided, they're thine own:
Heaven give thee a blessing with 'em; the best joys
That can in worldly shapes to man betide
Are fertile lands and a fair fruitful bride,
Of which I hope thou'rt sped.

SEBASTIAN   I hope so too sir.   205

MOLL
Father and son, I ha' done you simple service here.

188 *challenge* rival, or be the equivalent of
196 *those* sc. the eyes of judgment
205 *sped* provided; but (cf. previous line) to speed is to be sexually potent
206 *simple* pure, disinterested

SEBASTIAN
For which thou shalt not part, Moll, unrequited.

SIR ALEXANDER
Thou art a mad girl, and yet I cannot now
Condemn thee.

MOLL   Condemn me? troth and you should, sir,
I'd make you seek out one to hang in my room,   210
I'd give you the slip at gallows, and cozen the people.
Heard you this jest, my Lord?

LORD NOLAND   What is it, Jack?

MOLL
He was in fear his son would marry me,
But never dreamt that I would ne'er agree.

LORD NOLAND
Why? Thou hadst a suitor once, Jack, when wilt marry?   215

MOLL
Who, I, my Lord? I'll tell you when i'faith:
                When you shall hear
                Gallants void from sergeants' fear,
                Honesty and truth unslandered,
                Woman manned but never pandered,   220
                Cheators booted but not coached,
                Vessels older ere they're broached.
                If my mind be then not varied,
                Next day following I'll be married.

LORD NOLAND
This sounds like doomsday.

MOLL   Then were marriage best,   225
For if I should repent, I were soon at rest.

SIR ALEXANDER
In troth thou'rt a good wench, I'm sorry now
The opinion was so hard I conceived of thee.
Some wrongs I've done thee.

Enter TRAPDOOR

209 *and* if
222 *Vessels* sc. maidenheads

---

221 *Cheators booted but not coached.* (Cheates Q) Though Moll's general
    intention seems clear enough, the precise meaning of this line is not.
    'Booted', in addition to the obvious sense, can mean cured and also
    thrashed; 'coached' might mean trained. Perhaps she wants them made
    honest but not rich. A harlot is described as coming 'most commonly
    coached' in *A Mad World, My Masters*, III.iii, 47. 'Couched' might be
    preferred: cf. Epistle, 13 and III.i, 12. For *cheators*, see v.i, 301.

TRAPDOOR   Is the wind there now?
  'Tis time for me to kneel and confess first,   230
  For fear it come too late and my brains feel it.
  Upon my paws I ask you pardon, mistress.
MOLL
  Pardon? for what, sir? what has your rogueship done now?
TRAPDOOR
  I have been from time to time hired to confound you
  By this old gentleman.
MOLL   How?
TRAPDOOR   Pray forgive him,   235
  But may I counsel you, you should never do't.
  Many a snare to entrap your worship's life
  Have I laid privily, chains, watches, jewels,
  And when he saw nothing could mount you up,
  Four hollow-hearted angels he then gave you,   240
  By which he meant to trap you, I to save you.
SIR ALEXANDER
  To all which shame and grief in me cry guilty:
  Forgive me, now I cast the world's eyes from me,
  And look upon thee freely with mine own,
  I see the most of many wrongs before thee   245
  Cast from the jaws of envy and her people,
  And nothing foul but that. I'll never more
  Condemn by common voice, for that's the whore
  That deceives man's opinion, mocks his trust,
  Cozens his love, and makes his heart unjust.   250
MOLL
  Here be the angels, gentlemen, they were given me
  As a musician. I pursue no pity:
  Follow the law: and you can cuck me, spare not:
  Hang up my viol by me, and I care not.
SIR ALEXANDER
  So far I'm sorry, I'll thrice double 'em   255
  To make thy wrongs amends.
  Come, worthy friends, my honourable Lord,
  Sir Beauteous Ganymede, and noble Fitz-Allard,

236 *may I counsel you* if you take my advice
240 *hollow-hearted angels* i.e., with holes through the middle; cf.
    IV.i, 200
245 *thee* ed. (hee Q) *before thee* done to thee
246 *Cast* i.e., are cast, thrown at you
252 *pursue* seek
253 *and you can cuck me* if you can get me into a cucking-stool

And you kind gentlewomen, whose sparkling presence
Are glories set in marriage, beams of society,   260
For all your loves give lustre to my joys:
The happiness of this day shall be remembered
At the return of every smiling spring:
In my time now 'tis born, and may no sadness
Sit on the brows of men upon that day,   265
But as I am so all go pleased away.   [*Exeunt* OMNES]

EPILOGUS

[spoken by MOLL]

A painter having drawn with curious art
The picture of a woman (every part
Limned to the life) hung out the piece to sell:
People who passed along, viewing it well,
Gave several verdicts on it: some dispraised   5
The hair, some said the brows too high were raised,
Some hit her o'er the lips, misliked their colour,
Some wished her nose were shorter, some the eyes fuller;
Others said roses on her cheeks should grow,
Swearing they looked too pale, others cried no.   10
The workman, still as fault was found, did mend it
In hope to please all; but, this work being ended
And hung open at stall, it was so vile,
So monstrous and so ugly all men did smile
At the poor painter's folly. Such we doubt   15
Is this our comedy: some perhaps do flout
The plot, saying 'tis too thin, too weak, too mean;
Some for the person will revile the scene,
And wonder that a creature of her being
Should be the subject of a poet, seeing   20
In the world's eye none weighs so light: others look

260 *beams* sunbeams
  7 *hit ... o'er* directed their criticism toward
 11 *still as* each time

259 *gentlewomen* ed. (gentlewoman Q): addressed to the citizens' wives; *Are*
    in the following line is influenced by this plural.
264 *In my time*. Bowers amends to 'May time'; but Q is perfectly intelligible
    —Sir Alexander hopes the happiness will be remembered beyond his
    own time.

For all those base tricks published in a book
(Foul as his brains they flowed from) of cutpurses,
Of nips and foists, nasty, obscene discourses,
As full of lies, as empty of worth or wit,   25
For any honest ear, or eye, unfit.
And thus,
If we to every brain that's humorous
Should fashion scenes, we (with the painter) shall
In striving to please all, please none at all.   30
Yet for such faults, as either the writers' wit
Or negligence of the actors do commit,
Both crave your pardons: if what both have done
Cannot full pay your expectation,
The Roaring Girl herself, some few days hence,   35
Shall on this stage give larger recompense.
Which mirth that you may share in, herself does woo you,
And craves this sign, your hands to beckon her to you.

FINIS

---

23 *cutpurses* ed. (cutpurse Q)
28 *humorous* whimsical, full of humours or fancies

---

22 *a book*. The precise allusion is irrecoverable: Dekker's tracts on villainy
were quite late comers in a tradition which goes back at least as far as
John Awdeley's somewhat fanciful *Fraternity of Vagabonds* (1561).
There seems no need to suppose an allusion to a book about Moll herself. For the view that the book may be a lost tract by the author of
Martin Mark-All, see above, p. xv.
35–6 There has been much discussion about what these lines refer to (see
above, pp. xiiiff.). Though the assumption has been commonly made
that Mary Frith herself is the subject of them, it is possible that the
allusion is to the actor playing the part, who presumably would shortly
act again in another comedy on the same stage.

APPENDIX

Cant and Canting

This word *canting* seems to be derived from the Latin verb *canto*, which signifies in English 'to sing' or 'to make a sound with words', that's to say 'to speak'. And very aptly may *canting* take his derivation *a cantando* 'from singing' because amongst these beggarly consorts, that can play upon no better instruments, the language of *canting* is a kind of music and he that in such assemblies can *cant* best is counted the best musician. (Dekker, *English Villainies Discovered by Lanthorn and Candlelight*, i)

Dekker got most of his knowledge of underworld cant at second hand. His three tracts on roguery—*The Seven Deadly Sins of London* (1606), *The Bellman of London* and *Lanthorn and Candlelight* (both 1608)—were latecomers in a tradition of 'manifest detections' which began perhaps with Robert Copland's *Highway to the Spital-house* (1535) and has its more modern derivatives in extensive dictionaries of cant and slang. Dekker depended heavily on his predecessors, in particular on Thomas Harman's *A Caveat for Common Cursitors* (1566), a book which, according to S. R. (probably Samuel Rid), the somewhat peppery author of *Martin Mark-All* (1610), was out of date and inaccurate by the early seventeenth century. The third edition of *Lanthorn and Candlelight* (1612) conse-quently included a supplement called 'O per se O'—probably, but not certainly, by Dekker—expanding and occasionally silently correcting earlier information. Most of these tracts contain brief 'canter's dictionaries', which by and large confirm one another's definitions: the following glossary of cant words in *The Roaring Girl* is compiled, wherever possible, from Dekker's, with sub-stantive variants noted from other sources. The sigla used are as follows:

B: *The Bellman of London* (Dekker, 1608)
C: *A Caveat for Common Cursitors* (Thomas Harman, 1566)
F: *The Fraternity of Vagabonds* (John Awdeley, 1561)
L: *Lanthorn and Candlelight* (Dekker, 1608)
M: *Martin Mark-All, Beadle of Bridewell* (S. R., 1610)
N: *A Notable Discovery of Cozenage* (Robert Greene, 1591)
O: *O per se O* (Dekker?, 1612)

Angler: 'a limb of an upright-man ... in the day time, they beg
from house to house, not so much for relief, as to spy what lies
fit for their nets, which in the night following they fish for. The
rod they angle with is a staff of five or six foot in length, in which
within one inch of the top is a little hole bored quite through,
into which hole they put an iron hook, and with the same do they
angle at windows about midnight, the draught they pluck up
being apparel, sheets, coverlets, or whatsoever their iron hooks
can lay hold of' (B)

Ben, benar: good, better (L)

Ben cove: see under *Cove*

Bing: come, go (L)

Bing awast (or *avast*)*:* get you hence (L); steal away (O)

Boil: see under *Smoke*

Booze (or *bouse*)*:* drink (L)

Boozing ken: alehouse (L, O)

Borde: shilling (L)

Bung: purse (L); 'now used for a pocket, heretofore for a purse' (M)

Cackling cheat: cock or capon: see *Cheat*

Caster: cloak (L)

Cheat: thing. 'By joining of two simples do they make almost all
their compounds. As for example, *nab* in the canting tongue is a
head, and *nab cheat* is a hat or a cap. Which word *cheat*, being
coupled to other words, stands in very good stead and does
excellent service ... a *muffling cheat* signifies a napkin, a *belly
cheat* an apron, a *grunting cheat* a pig, a *cackling cheat* a cock or
capon, a *quacking cheat* a duck, ... and so may that word be
married to many others besides' (L). The word is of course also
used in the play in its standard sense

Cheator: 'The Cheating Law, or the art of winning money by false
dice: those that practise this study call themselves *cheators*, the
dice *cheaters*, and the money which they purchase *cheats*' (B).
For a more detailed explanation, see F

Cheats (*chats, chates*)*:* the gallows (L, C). 'Here he [the Bellman]
mistakes both the simple word, because he found it so printed,
not knowing the true original thereof, and also in the com-
pound. As for *chates* it should be *cheats*, which word is used
generally for things ... so that if you will make a word for
gallows, you must put thereto this word, *trining*, which signifies
hanging; and so *trining-cheat* is as much as to say "hanging-things",
or the gallows, and not *chates*' (M)

Cloyer: see under *Figging-Law*; '*priggers, filchers* and *cloyers* (being
all in English stealers)' (O)

Couch a hogshead: lie down asleep (L). 'This phrase is like an almanac that is out of date: now the Dutch word *slope* is with them used, "to sleep", and *liggen*, "to lie down" ' (M)

Cove, Cuffin: 'The word *cove* or *cofe* or *cuffin* signifies a man, a fellow, etc., but differs something in his property according as it meets with other words, for a gentleman is called a *gentry cove* or *cofe*, a good fellow is a *ben cofe*, a churl is called a *queer cuffin* (*queer* signifies naught and *cuffin*, as I said before, a man) and in canting they term a Justice of the Peace (because he punisheth them, belike) by no other name than by *queer cuffin*, that's to say a churl or a naughty man' (L)

Cramp-ring: hand-cuff; and see under *Scour*

Curber: 'The Curbing Law [teaches] how to hook goods out of a window . . . He that hooks is called the *curber* . . . The hook is the *curb*' (B) cf. *Angler*

Cut ben (*benar*) *whids:* speak good (better) words (L); tell the truth (M)

Darkmans: the night (L)

Dell: 'A dell is a young wench, . . . but as yet not spoiled of her maidenhead ["able for generation, and not yet known or broken" (C)]. These dells are reserved as dishes for the upright-men, for none but they must have the first taste of them' (B)

Deuse a vill (or *deuceville*): the country (L)

Dock: lie with

Doxy: whore (O); 'his woman . . . which he calleth his altham, if she be his wife, and if she be his harlot, she is called his doxy' (F); 'these doxies be broken and spoiled of their maidenhead by the upright-men, and then they have their name of doxies, and not afore' (C)

Fadoodling: copulating

Fambles: hands (L)

Figging-Law: 'Cutting of purses and picking of pockets' (N): 'In making of which law, two persons have the chief voices, that is to say, the cutpurse and the pickpocket, and all the branches of this law reach to none but them and such as are made free denizens of their incorporation . . . He that cuts the purse is called the *nip*, he that is half with him is the *snap* or the *cloyer* . . . He that picks the pocket is called a *foist*, he that faceth the man is the *stale*' (B)

Foist: see under *Figging-Law*

Gage: a quart pot (L)

Gentry cuffin: see under *Cove*

Ging: company, gang (Dekker, *Penny-Wise, Pound-Foolish*)

Glaziers: eyes (L)

Goll: hand (Dekker, *The Wonderful Year*)

Grunt(l)ing cheat: pig; see *Cheat*

Hartmans (or *harmans*): the stocks (L)

Heave a booth (or *bough*): rob a booth (L)

Ken: house (L)

Kinchin mort: 'Kinchin-morts are girls of a year or two old, which the *morts* (their mothers) carry at their backs in their slates (which in the canting-tongue are sheets)' (B)

Lap: buttermilk or whey (L)

Lib: sleep (L)

Libken: a house to lie in (L); a house to lodge people (M)

Lifter: 'The Lifting Law ... teacheth a kind of lifting of goods clean away' (B)

Lightmans: the day

Maund: to ask (F, L); to beg (M, O)

Maunder, maunderer: beggar (O)

Mill: to steal or rob (L)

Mort: woman (esp. one who has fallen from a better state) (L)

Mutton: food for lust, hence a prostitute

Nab: head (L)

Niggle: to company with a woman (L). 'This word is not now used, but *wapping*, and thereof comes the name *wapping-morts*, whores' (M)

Nip (noun): see under *Figging-Law*

Nip a bung: to cut a purse (L)

Pad: a way, highway (L)

Palliard: 'he that goeth in a patched cloak' (F); some are 'natural' (born to the trade), some 'artificial': the latter 'carrieth about him the great *cleyme* [an artificially induced sore] to stir compassion up in people's hearts' (O)

Pannum (*pannam* or *pennam*): bread (L)

Peck: meat (L). '*Peck* is not meat, but *peckage. Peck* is taken to eat or bite' (M)

Pedlar's French: 'that canting language which is to be found among none but beggars' (B), 'invented to th'intent that, albeit any spies should secretly steal into their companies to discover them, they might freely utter their minds one to another, yet avoid that danger' (L)

Poplars (or *popler*): porridge (C), pottage (L)

Priggard (*prigger* or *prigman*): a stealer generally (O), but applied especially to *priggers of prancers* (horse-thieves) (N). But 'a prigman goeth with a stick ... to steal clothes off the hedge' (F)

Quacking-cheat: duck; see under *Cheat*

Queer: naught, naughty (L)

Queer cuffin: see under *Cove*

Rom-booze (or *rom-bouse*)*:* wine (L). 'This word [*rom* or *room*] is always taken in the best sense, to show a thing extraordinary or excellent' (M)

Rom-ville: London (L), or more generally a great town (M)

Ruffler: 'a ruffler goeth with a weapon to seek service, saying he hath been a servitor in the wars, and beggeth for his relief' (F). 'The ruffler and the upright-man are so like in conditions, that you would swear them brothers: they walk with cudgels alike; they profess arms alike ... These commonly are fellows that have stood aloof in the wars, and whilst others fought, they took their heels and ran away from their captain, or else they would have been serving-men, whom for their behaviour no man would trust with a livery' (B)

Ruffmans: hedges, woods or bushes (L). 'Not the hedge or bushes as heretofore; but now the eavesing of houses or roofs. *Cragmans* is now used for the hedge' (M)

Salomon: the Mass (L), used chiefly in oaths

Scour the (*queer*) *cramp-ring:* to wear bolts or fetters (C)

Shells: money (B)

Shifter: cozener (F)

Skelder: to live by begging, especially by passing oneself off as a wounded or disbanded soldier

Skew: all authorities agree that this means a cup (C, L, M); but in *The Roaring Girl* it is used as a verb, meaning to drink

Slate: sheet; see under *Kinchin mort*

Smoke: 'The spying of this villainy is called smoking or boiling' (B)

Snap: 'he that is half with him [the nip]' (N): see under *Figging-Law* and *Upright-man*

Stale: see under *Figging-Law*

Stall: to make or ordain (L): so

Stalled to the rogue: 'I do stall thee to the rogue by virtue of this sovereign English liquor, so that henceforth it shall be lawful for thee to cant, that is to say to be a vagabond and to beg' (B)

Stalling- (or *stuling-*) *ken:* house for receiving stolen goods (L)

Stamps: legs (L)

Strike: 'the act doing' (in figging-law) (N)

Strommel (or *strummel*)*:* straw (L)

Synagogue: an assembly of thieves (?)

Trine: hang (L); see also under *Cheats*

Upright-man: 'a sturdy big-boned knave, that never walks but (like a commander) with a short truncheon in his hand, which he calls his filchman. At markets, fairs, and other meetings his voice among beggars is of the same sound that a constable's is of, it is not to be controlled' (B). 'This man is of so much authority that, meeting with any of his profession, he may call them to account, and command a share or snap unto himself of all that they have gained by their trade in one month' (F)

Wap: see under *Niggle*

Whip-jack: 'Another sort of knaves . . . are called whip-jacks, who talk of nothing but fights at sea, piracies, drownings and ship-wrecks' (B). 'These fresh-water mariners, their ships were drowned in the plain of Salisbury' (C)

Wild dell: a dell born to the position: 'those such as are born or begotten under a hedge' (B)

Wild rogue: 'one that is born a rogue . . . begotten in barn or bushes, and from his infancy traded up in treachery'; 'a rogue is neither so stout or hardy as the upright-man' (C). He 'is a spirit that cares not in what circle he rises, nor into the company of what devils he falls: in his swaddling clouts is he marked to be a villain, and in his breeding is instructed to be so . . . These wild rogues (like wild geese) keep in flocks, and all the day loiter in fields, if the weather be warm, and at brick-kilns, or else disperse themselves in cold weather, to rich men's doors, and at night have their meetings in barns or other out-places' (B)

A selection of these various tracts (not all printed complete) was compiled by A. V. Judges and published in 1930 as *The Elizabethan Underworld*; some have been reprinted by the Early English Text Society (1869) and the New Shakspere Society (1880). Dekker's (without *O per se O*) were included in Grosart's edition of the non-dramatic works (1884–86) and in an edition by O. Smeaton (1904). *Lanthorn and Candlelight* has lately been reprinted complete, with *O per se O*, in a collection of Dekker's tales and tracts edited by E. D. Pendry (1967).

Printed in Great Britain by
The Garden City Press Limited,
Letchworth, Hertfordshire, SG6 1JS